SAVING ENDANGERED SPECIES

THE
FLORIDA PANTHER
Help Save This Endangered Species!

Marty Fletcher and
Glenn Scherer

MyReportLinks.com Books

an imprint of

Enslow Publishers, Inc. E

Box 398, 40 Industrial Road
Berkeley Heights, NJ 07922
USA

MyReportLinks.com Books, an imprint of Enslow Publishers, Inc. MyReportLinks®
is a registered trademark of Enslow Publishers, Inc.

Library of Congress Cataloging-in-Publication Data

Fletcher, Marty.
  The Florida panther : help save this endangered species! / Marty Fletcher and Glenn Scherer.
     p. cm.— (Saving endangered species)
  Includes bibliographical references and index.
  ISBN-10: 1-59845-034-4
  1. Florida panther—Juvenile literature. I. Scherer, Glenn. II. Title. III. Series.
  QL737.C23F62 2006
  599.75'2409759—dc22
                                    2005034712
  ISBN-13: 978-1-59845-034-7

Printed in the United States of America

3 1969 01955 5878

10 9 8 7 6 5 4 3 2

To Our Readers:
Through the purchase of this book, you and your library gain access to the Report Links that specifically
back up this book.
The Publisher will provide access to the Report Links that back up this book and will keep these Report
Links up to date on **www.myreportlinks.com** for five years from the book's first publication date.
We have done our best to make sure all Internet addresses in this book were active and appropriate when
we went to press. However, the author and the Publisher have no control over, and assume no liability
for, the material available on those Internet sites or on other Web sites they may link to.
The usage of the MyReportLinks.com Books Web site is subject to the terms and conditions stated on the
Usage Policy Statement on **www.myreportlinks.com**.
A password may be required to access the Report Links that back up this book. The password is found
on the bottom of page 4 of this book.
Any comments or suggestions can be sent by e-mail to comments@myreportlinks.com or to the address
on the back cover.

♻ Enslow Publishers, Inc., is committed to printing our books on recycled paper. The paper in every
book contains 10% to 30% post-consumer waste (PCW). The cover board on the outside of each book
contains 100% PCW. Our goal is to do our part to help young people and the environment too!

Photo Credits: © Corel Corporation, pp. 3, 10, 20–21, 27, 35, 40, 46–47, 67, 71, 93, 97; © Digital
Vision, pp. 1, 76, 114; Audubon of Florida, p. 107; Big Cat Rescue, p. 48; Defenders of Wildlife,
pp. 23, 91; *EcoFlorida*, p. 52; Enslow Publishers, Inc., p. 5; Florida Museum of Natural History, p. 73;
Ibiblio.org, p. 39; IUCN, pp. 80, 86; MyReportLinks.com Books, p. 4; National Park Service, pp. 41, 43,
50, 55; National Resources Defense Council, p. 103; National Wildlife Federation, p. 16; PBS, p. 53;
Photos.com, p. 33; Public Library of Science, p. 37; San Diego Zoo, p. 89; The Florida Panther Society,
p. 105; The Nature Conservancy, p. 95; The Panther Project, p. 109; The Sierra Club, p. 100; The State
of Florida, pp. 17, 31; U.S. Fish and Wildlife Service, pp. 14, 25, 30, 62, 65, 82, 84, 117; U.S. Geological
Survey, p. 12; Union of Concerned Scientists, p. 101; University of Florida, pp. 60, 69; University of
Tennessee, p. 58; Wildlife Conservation Society, p. 74; World Wildlife Fund, p. 111.

Cover Photo: © Digital Vision.

CONTENTS

About MyReportLinks.com Books   4

Florida Panther Range Map   5

Florida Panther Facts   6

1▶ The Race to Save the Florida Panther **9**

2▶ All About Florida's Big Cat **29**

3▶ Threats to Survival **57**

4▶ Protecting the Panther **79**

5▶ The Florida Panther Today **99**

**6▶ Hope for the Florida Panther
      and Humanity** **113**

The Endangered and
    Threatened Wildlife List **117**

Report Links **118**

Glossary **120**

Chapter Notes **122**

Further Reading **125**

Index **126**

MyReportLinks.com Books
Great Books, Great Links, Great for Research!

The Internet sites featured in this book can save you hours of research time. These Internet sites—we call them **"Report Links"**—are constantly changing, but we keep them up to date on our Web site.

When you see this "Approved Web Site" logo, you will know that we are directing you to a great Internet site that will help you with your research.

Give it a try! Type http://www.myreportlinks.com into your browser, click on the series title and enter the password, then click on the book title, and scroll down to the Report Links listed for this book.

The Report Links will bring you to great source documents, photographs, and illustrations. MyReportLinks.com Books save you time, feature Report Links that are kept up to date, and make report writing easier than ever! A complete listing of the Report Links can be found on pages 118–119 at the back of the book.

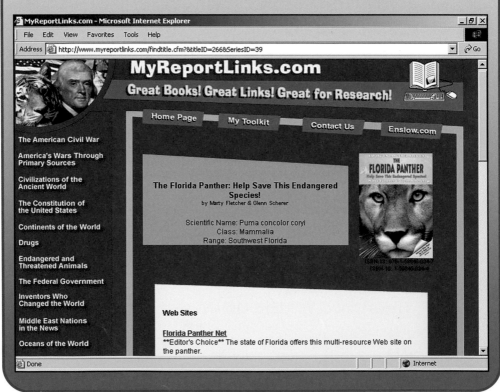

Please see "To Our Readers" on the copyright page for important information about this book, the MyReportLinks.com Web site, and the Report Links that back up this book.

Please enter SFP2815 if asked for a password.

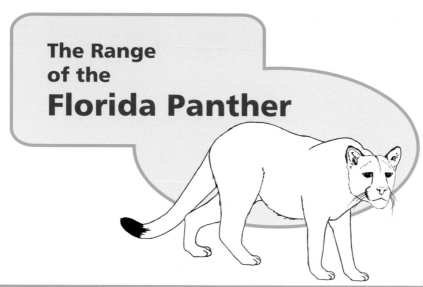

The Range of the Florida Panther

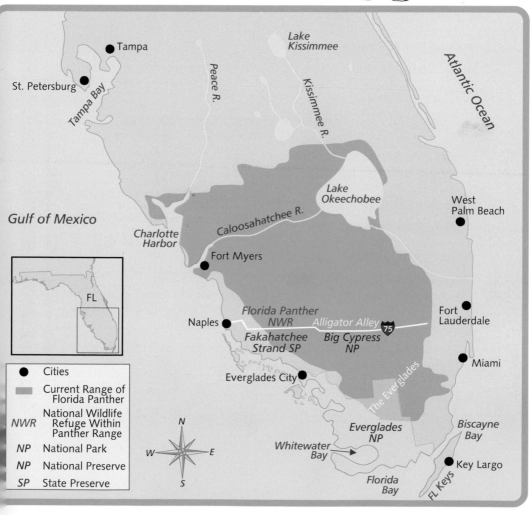

Tampa

St. Petersburg

Tampa Bay

Peace R.

Lake Kissimmee

Kissimmee R.

Atlantic Ocean

Gulf of Mexico

Lake Okeechobee

West Palm Beach

Charlotte Harbor

Caloosahatchee R.

Fort Myers

FL

Florida Panther NWR

Naples

Alligator Alley

Fort Lauderdale

75

Fakahatchee Strand SP

Big Cypress NP

Everglades City

Miami

The Everglades

	Cities
	Current Range of Florida Panther
NWR	National Wildlife Refuge Within Panther Range
NP	National Park
NP	National Preserve
SP	State Preserve

N

W — E

S

Everglades NP

Whitewater Bay

Biscayne Bay

Key Largo

FL Keys

Florida Bay

FLORIDA PANTHER FACTS

▶ **Scientific Name**

Puma concolor coryi

▶ **Size**

Length, 6 to 7 feet (1.8 to 2.2 meters) from tip of nose to tip of tail. Height, 24 to 28 inches (61 to 71 centimeters) at shoulders.

▶ **Weight**

Adult males range from 99 to 154 pounds (45 to 70 kilograms), and adult females from 66 to 99 pounds (30 to 45 kilograms).

▶ **Leaping Distance**

Panthers can jump up to 14.7 feet (4.5 meters) to make a kill.

▶ **Historic Range**

North from Florida, through Georgia, South Carolina, and into Tennessee. Westward through Mississippi, Alabama, Arkansas, and Louisiana. The Florida panther likely once mixed with and mated with the Texas subspecies of cougar.

▶ **Current Range**

Southwest Florida

▶ **Current Habitat**

Once thought to prefer upland forests, Florida panthers are now known by conservationists to be habitat generalists. They live in a wide variety of habitats but in particular need ground vegetation for their dens and daybeds. They have been able to survive in almost any habitat that offers enough prey and cover.

▶ **Diet**

Florida panthers are carnivores, or meat-eaters, who eat mostly live white-tailed deer and wild hogs, but also armadillos, raccoons, rabbits, rats, birds, and even an occasional alligator. They sometimes eat carrion, or dead animals.

▶ Amount of Meat Adult Panther Can Eat at One Sitting

19.8 to 30.1 pounds (9 to 14 kilograms)

▶ Sexual Maturity

Males mature at about 3 years of age and females at about 1.5 to 2.5 years of age.

▶ Litter

One to four kittens, usually born in the spring

▶ Gestation Period

About three months

▶ Age When Kittens Leave Mother

Between 1.5 to 2 years old

▶ Life Span

Average of 12 years; one is known to have lived 16 years.

▶ Date Protected

First protected under Florida state law in 1958. First federally listed as endangered on March 11, 1967, as part of the Endangered Species Preservation Act of 1966. Listed as endangered under the United States Endangered Species Act of 1973 at the time of its passage.

▶ Population

Approximately 70 to 100 remaining in the wild

▶ Major Threats

Habitat loss, habitat fragmentation and degradation (leading to territorial fights to the death among adult males; also results in insufficient prey), collisions with automobiles, inbreeding, disease, mercury poisoning, and poor cooperation between various levels of government trying to save the Florida panther

The panther deserves to live. . . . The panther belongs in Florida. The panther is Florida.

Charles Fergus

Chapter 1 ▶

THE RACE TO SAVE THE FLORIDA PANTHER

The year was 1973. The Florida panther had just been listed as an endangered species under the newly passed Endangered Species Act. At the time, scientists were not sure that the Florida panther, a North American cougar subspecies, was not already extinct.

Sightings of the panther in the tangled cypress swamps, pinelands, and steamy mixed hardwood hammock islands of South Florida were extremely rare, uncertain, and controversial. The few panthers that had been found dead or had been photographed were not thought to be true Florida panthers by some biologists. The animals were believed to be captive panthers raised from kittens as pets, which, when full grown, had been released into the wild to fend for themselves by uncaring owners.

The World Wildlife Fund, in an effort to settle the controversy once and for all, hired Roy McBride, a Texan and one of the world's most skilled animal trackers, to go deep into the South Florida wilderness to find a pure-blooded Florida panther. McBride was not only a top tracker but

With ever-diminishing habitat, the elusive big cat known as the Florida panther is in a fight for its survival.

also had a degree in biology. He was already famous for finding the last remaining Mexican wolves.

Within weeks of his assignment, McBride successfully treed an old female Florida panther along Fisheating Creek, west of Lake Okeechobee, Florida.[1] But the big cat's physical condition was hardly promising. The pathetic animal was old, tick infested, just skin and bones, and had worn-down teeth. While McBride's discovery proved that there were still Florida panthers in the wild, it did not prove that there were any young, healthy panthers left that could breed and save the species. That fact could only be determined by intense scientific study. Unfortunately, for the next few years, little was done to save the Florida panther. Though a detailed government recovery plan was written, no real action happened in the field.

Panther Research Takes Off

Jump forward in time to February 1981. A tiny expedition of federal and Florida wildlife officials, led by tracker Roy McBride, trudged into the knee-deep waters of southwestern Florida's Fakahatchee Strand State Preserve—a remote swamp and waterway that drains the 2,400-square-mile Big Cypress Swamp. The Fakahatchee Strand is a place that most Americans probably would not even recognize as being part of the

▲ *Winter in the swamps of the Fakahatchee Strand finds cypress trees without their leaves.*

United States. Its intensely hot subtropical climate causes plants to grow very quickly, making it look like a dense, tangled jungle in Africa. Immense royal palms and lush ferns rise from the forest floor. Moss-covered bald cypress trees stand with their gnarled roots sometimes submerged beneath the water. The largest concentration and variety of wild orchids anywhere in the United States are found here, not growing out of the ground, but hung like festive Christmas ornaments on the trunks and branches of the cypress trees. The wood stork, Florida black bear, mangrove fox squirrel, and Everglades mink have all been found within the Fakahatchee Strand State Preserve. It was time to see if the Florida panther could be added to this list of creatures.

The First Step

Early on the morning of February 10, 1981, McBride released his trained cougar hounds, hunting dogs that he called his "professors of pantherology" into the Fakahatchee Strand.[2] At 8:25 A.M., the silence of the swamp was shattered by the excited yowls, yelps, and barks of the hunting dogs, a sign that they were on the trail of a large game animal. McBride radioed the news to the other members of his team, who were waiting nearby. On hearing the report, the rest of the team rushed into the steamy mosquito-infested swamp and began moving quickly toward McBride and his dogs. Ken Alvarez, in his book *The Twilight of the Panther,* describes what happened next:

> [The team] went sloshing through the dense, tropical undergrowth, sweating heavily in the humid air. Spurred on by excitement, they reached McBride and the dogs by 10:30 a.m.
>
> Peering down from the limb of an oak tree, 15 feet above the ground, was the first wild [Florida] panther any of them (with the exception of McBride) had ever seen alive. Heads tilted back, they looked with wide-eyed fixation, aware that the cornered cat represented the first step in a journey of understanding that all hoped might insure the presence of panthers in Florida [for centuries to come]. A supreme

challenge and dream of wildlife professionals—the coaxing of an endangered creature back from the abyss of extinction—was embodied in the frightened animal clinging to a limb above their heads.[3]

From that moment forward, the race was on to save the endangered Florida panther. The team of scientists jumped into action. McBride loaded a tranquilizer dart into his gun and shot the panther in the rump. The male panther stayed on its high treetop perch but grew drowsy over the next few minutes. Chris Belden, a Florida Game and Fresh Water Fish Commission biologist, decided to rescue the drugged animal before it toppled from the tree, possibly injuring itself. But

▲ U.S. Fish and Wildlife Service biologists collect samples from a tranquilized panther to test for mercury exposure and disease.

as Belden climbed a rope, he got a surprise. The dozing cat fell, and both man and beast crashed to the ground. Fortunately, neither was hurt. The big cat, though heavily drugged, still had some fight left in it. It began to run weakly. Roy McBride chased after the panther, caught it by the tail, and gave it another shot of tranquilizer that left it unconscious.

In the next half hour, the team of researchers weighed the sleeping animal. It came in at 120 pounds (54 kilograms), about average for today's Florida panthers. Blood and fecal samples were taken. Then, most importantly, a radio collar was attached to the panther's neck. In the coming months, the scientists would do something no other biologists had ever done before: They would be able to follow every movement of a Florida panther as it prowled through the trackless wilds of the Fakahatchee Strand.

Counting the Last Florida Panthers

Within days, another panther was found by McBride, and more followed. Guesses were made about the size of the surviving Florida panther population, ranging from as low as thirty animals to as high as fifty. Unfortunately, neither of these population figures gave anyone much confidence about the Florida panther's chances for survival. Such a small population would be hard to

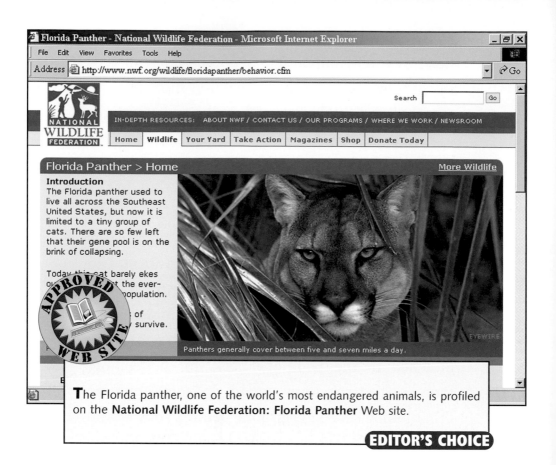

The Florida panther, one of the world's most endangered animals, is profiled on the **National Wildlife Federation: Florida Panther** Web site.

EDITOR'S CHOICE

maintain even under natural conditions. But the Florida panther was not living under natural conditions. It was embattled from all sides. Its numbers were being steadily eroded by loss of habitat and encroaching human development, collisions with cars, disease, and other threats to its existence.

▷ Early Efforts to Save the Panther

Still, the biologists hoped that a unified federal and Florida state government effort could lead to the panther's recovery. From the early 1980s onward, the National Park Service, U.S. Fish and Wildlife Service, Florida Game Commission, and Florida Department of Natural Resources, along with private groups like the Florida Audubon Society and the Florida Panther Society, worked diligently to save the Florida panther.

No effort to bring back a large predator so near to extinction had ever been tried before, so the slow process was filled with mistakes, false starts, delays, dead ends, and disagreements. In the process, the Florida panther became one of the

http://www.flheritage.com/facts/symbols/images/symbols/panther.jpg - Microsoft Internet Explorer

File   Edit   View   Favorites   Tools   Help

Address http://www.flheritage.com/facts/symbols/images/symbols/panther.jpg

Students from Florida voted in 1982 to name the Florida panther the state animal. Learn more at **Florida State Symbols: The State Animal.**

EDITOR'S CHOICE

most researched and closely watched animal species on earth.

The attempts to save the panther also caught the public imagination. In 1982, Florida school-children were asked to select a state animal. They chose the Florida panther, outvoting both the alligator and the manatee.[4] Since then, the panther has become an important state symbol, and the state's professional hockey team bears its name.

Today, the Florida panther remains the most endangered of all the subspecies of cougar in North or South America. But its numbers have steadily risen to between seventy and one hundred panthers. To biologists, this is a sign for cautious hope—cautious because it will take many more years of diligent work to safely guide the Florida panther back from the brink of extinction. Without the support of people all around the country, the Florida panther could still disappear from the world forever within just a few decades.

Why Save the Florida Panther?

The Florida panther is said by some conservationists to belong to a group of endangered animals known as the "charismatic megafauna." These are big animals that are few in number, on the brink of extinction, that attract a huge amount of public attention and support for preservation. Included in this group are the grizzly bear, whooping crane, spotted owl, red wolf, blue whale, and all kinds of sea turtles. These are creatures that people feel an urge to protect.

While it is hard to get most people excited about rescuing tiny fish like snail darters, the Dismal Swamp Southeastern shrew, or rare mold beetles, the charismatic megafauna almost always find a big public following. This concern for megafauna does much more than protect Florida panthers and grizzly bears. It helps protect the entire habitat in which those animals live.

▶ Under the Umbrella

The Florida panther is known as an umbrella species. The survival of such a species means that the plants and animals in its environment will also survive. To save the Florida panther in the wild, it is also necessary to save the entire environment in which it lives. That means protecting South Florida's prehistoric-looking landscape of saw grass marsh and cypress swamp where the big cat finds cover. It means protecting pinelands and hardwood hammocks where the panther hunts. It also means protecting the sloughs (pronounced *slews*), winding streams and shallow pockets of water where panthers come to drink and alligators stay in midwinter's dry season. Saving the panther also means saving the last few surviving great bald cypress trees, seven-hundred-year-old giants that

Florida panthers would rather live in drier areas than the marshes and swamps of the Everglades, but habitat loss has forced the big cats into places where people are less likely to be.

amazingly escaped lumbermen who once sought their wood to make everything from pickle barrels to PT boats.

We cannot save large, charismatic animals like the Florida panther without saving their habitat. The Endangered Species Act of 1973 requires protection of critical habitat, which is the entire functioning ecosystem that an endangered animal lives in. In the case of Florida panthers, however, the federal government has not designated critical habitat for the animals, and their habitat consists equally of public and private lands. The public lands in South Florida where they live include Big Cypress National Preserve, Corkscrew Swamp, Everglades National Park, and the Florida Panther National Wildlife Refuge.

Keeping Habitats Healthy

There is another reason why saving a big animal like the Florida panther is important. In *Solitary Spirits,* author Dennis Olson writes, "The distribution of the cougar can be thought of as a general indicator of the health of the land."[5] In other words, if big predators like panthers are healthy and thriving, then the rest of the surrounding environment and its many plant and animal species are likely to be doing well, too. That is because large predators like the Florida panther are at the very top of the food chain.

Defenders Magazine - Defenders of Wildlife - Summer 2005 Issue - Microsoft Internet Explorer

File   Edit   View   Favorites   Tools   Help

Address http://www.defenders.org/defendersmag/issues/summer05/cats.html   Go

DEFENDERS OF WILDLIFE

ABOUT US   PUBLICATIONS   NEWSROOM   WILDLIFE   HABITAT   DONATE

Defenders

SUMMER 2005

DEFENDERS IN ACTION
Conservation News from Defenders

The Fall of the Cat of God
A real estate boom threatens the rare Florida panther

By Bill Updike

Dump trucks line the road fronting the offices of the Florida Panther National Wildlife Refuge on this sunny spring morning in southwestern Florida. The trucks, sitting at a stoplight on Highway 951 in Naples, are carrying limestone, trees and shrubs out of the forests, prairies and swamps surrounding the 26,400-acre refuge. The contents are headed for the dump-- the final resting place of much of Florida's natural habitats

© USFWS

Panther Threats, a Web page from Defenders of Wildlife, offers a link to this article about the threat that real-estate development poses to the panthers' already-dwindling habitat.

At the bottom of the food chain are the tiniest plants and insects, which are then eaten by bigger animals, which in turn are eaten by bigger animals. If any of the lower part of the food chain collapses—if a plant or animal goes extinct in an ecosystem—then every other link up the chain may be harmed.

If, for example, real-estate developers in South Florida build houses where pinelands once grew, then the white-tailed deer that browse the foliage and twigs in those forests might disappear. And if the deer die out, then the panthers that feed on them might go hungry and die of malnutrition. Likewise, if a toxic pollutant such as mercury is found in a plant species and that plant is then eaten by small animals, which in turn are eaten by bigger animals, the amount of toxic mercury concentrated in the bigger animal's fat increases dramatically and can be deadly. That is why the protection of a big predator at the top of the food chain such as the Florida panther also protects most, if not all, of the other animals and plants in the ecosystem.

The Florida panther has another key role to play. It naturally controls population explosions among its prey. Without the Florida panther, raccoons, deer, and wild hogs might reproduce out of control. "People don't understand how important panthers are," says Larry Richardson of the U.S. Fish and Wildlife Service (USFWS). "Everybody lives under the panthers' umbrella. If you protect the acreage they need, you have protected all the other animals."[6]

▶ Be Part of the Florida Panther Comeback

The more people who understand the risks that Florida panthers face, the more likely they will be to contribute money and time to the effort to save this species.

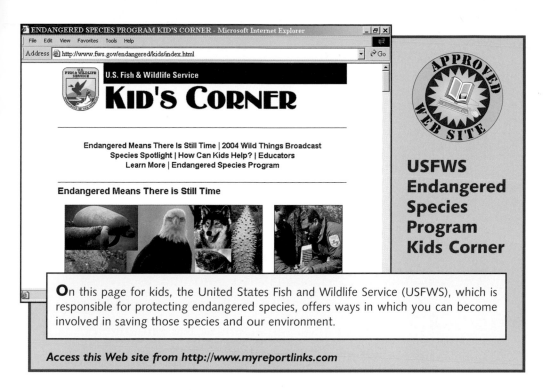

ENDANGERED SPECIES PROGRAM KID'S CORNER - Microsoft Internet Explorer

File   Edit   View   Favorites   Tools   Help

Address   http://www.fws.gov/endangered/kids/index.html   Go

U.S. Fish & Wildlife Service

KID'S CORNER

Endangered Means There Is Still Time | 2004 Wild Things Broadcast
Species Spotlight | How Can Kids Help? | Educators
Learn More | Endangered Species Program

Endangered Means There is Still Time

On this page for kids, the United States Fish and Wildlife Service (USFWS), which is responsible for protecting endangered species, offers ways in which you can become involved in saving those species and our environment.

Access this Web site from http://www.myreportlinks.com

USFWS Endangered Species Program Kids Corner

You can play a huge and influential role in doing just that. School projects focused on the Florida panther's plight can help end public apathy and build support for this endangered species. By educating your friends, family, community, and government officials about the panther, you can help bring attention to the many important environmental problems that are endangering this big cat and threatening many other species around the country. That is because an understanding of the panther's problems requires an understanding of more general ecological concepts and environmental threats such as urban sprawl, power-plant air pollution, and the negative effects of highways and cars on wildlife.

There are many ways to become involved in saving the Florida panther. Working with the Friends of the Florida Panther Refuge or the Florida Panther Society, you can start a Florida panther preservation campaign in your school. Letter-writing campaigns can produce results as well. For example, you might launch a letter-writing campaign in your school that seeks to convince elected officials to continue to protect endangered species, especially by not watering down the rules and regulations of the Endangered Species Act of 1973, which some in Congress are now trying to do.

Saving Nature for Our Sake

There is a final reason to save the Florida panther. This animal is unique on earth. A look into the panther's eyes is a look into a whole other universe with which we humans are unfamiliar and unacquainted. In his book *Swamp Screamer,* Charles Fergus writes,

> When I needed to remind myself that there was more to Florida than shopping malls, golfing communities, citrus groves, condominium-lined beaches . . . restaurants, bars, marinas, [and] gasoline stations . . . I would go to Fakahatchee Strand.[7]

In that wild place, Fergus says, he could walk peacefully through wild nature looking for signs of the Florida panther. And he could experience the magic of the natural world, watching "a thin morning mist swirled among the trees; the sun, boring through the vapor," noticing "a dew-covered spiderweb," observing lizards as they scurried across the path, or seeing flitting butterflies, "pumpkin-orange ones, ornate black-and-yellow

▲ Very few people have been lucky enough to see a Florida panther in the wild. For some, it is enough just knowing the big cats are there, free to roam. It is up to us to make sure that the species survives.

zebra butterflies, browns, whites, yellows, blues, grays," or smelling "the mingled perfumes of flowers in the air," or hearing "a thunderhead murmuring on the horizon."[8]

Fergus saw no sign of the Florida panther on his many hikes in the Fakahatchee Strand. But that does not matter to him. Just knowing that the big cat is out there, stalking a white-tailed deer or bedding down beneath an umbrella of palmetto leaves, enriches his experience of nature. "The panther deserves to live: if not for its sake alone, then for ours," concludes Fergus. "The panther belongs in Florida. The panther is Florida."[9] Without it, our world would be a poorer, less wonder-filled place.

Chapter 2

ALL ABOUT FLORIDA'S BIG CAT

America's elusive cougars are called by many regional and local names. Cougars in various parts of the United States have been called mountain lions, pumas, catamounts (cats-of-the-mountain), ghost cats, king cats, devil cats, deer tigers, yellow tigers, red tigers, screamers, and of course, panthers.[1]

But though this big American cat is known by many names, and though it is found as far north as Canada and as far south as Argentina, it is rarely ever seen by people. The cougar's mysteriousness, along with its reputation as a fierce and deadly predator and other misconceptions, may be what has caused many people to fear and misunderstand this magnificent animal. These fears and misunderstandings have led to the extermination and steady decline in cougar numbers over recent centuries.

American Indians also had many names for the cougar. The Seminole of Florida called the Florida panther *coo-wah-chobee,* or "big cat." The southeastern Cherokee called the panther *Klandagi,* or

▲ The Florida panther's reputation as a fierce predator has led many people to fear it, even though there has never been an attack by panthers on humans in Florida.

"Lord of the Forest," while the Chickasaw people called it *Ko-icto,* or the "Cat of God." All these names show the great respect that American Indians had for cougars.[2]

Scientists Name the Panther

Christopher Columbus was among the first Europeans to catch a glimpse of North American panthers in 1502, identifying them in his journals as *leones,* or lions.[3] Scientists now classify all North and South American cougars as *Puma concolor,* which means "mighty magic animal of one color." The term *puma* comes from the Spanish through a Quechua Indian word. *Felis concolor,* "cat of one color," was the name first given them in 1771 by the Swedish naturalist Carolus Linnaeus. Linnaeus was among the first naturalists to classify animals

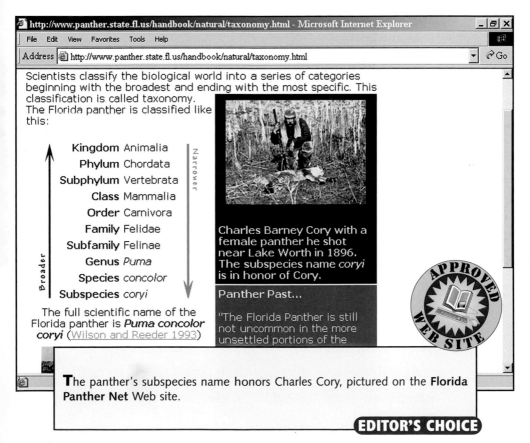

http://www.panther.state.fl.us/handbook/natural/taxonomy.html - Microsoft Internet Explorer

File   Edit   View   Favorites   Tools   Help

Address http://www.panther.state.fl.us/handbook/natural/taxonomy.html

Scientists classify the biological world into a series of categories beginning with the broadest and ending with the most specific. This classification is called taxonomy.
The Florida panther is classified like this:

Kingdom Animalia
Phylum Chordata
Subphylum Vertebrata
Class Mammalia
Order Carnivora
Family Felidae
Subfamily Felinae
Genus *Puma*
Species *concolor*
Subspecies *coryi*

Narrower
Broader

The full scientific name of the Florida panther is **Puma concolor coryi** (Wilson and Reeder 1993)

Charles Barney Cory with a female panther he shot near Lake Worth in 1896. The subspecies name *coryi* is in honor of Cory.

Panther Past...

"The Florida Panther is still not uncommon in the more unsettled portions of the

APPROVED WEB SITE

The panther's subspecies name honors Charles Cory, pictured on the **Florida Panther Net** Web site.

EDITOR'S CHOICE

scientifically. He sent his assistants from Europe around the world to identify and describe the earth's plants and animals.

The Florida panther was first described as a subspecies of cougar and given its own scientific name by naturalist and hunter Charles B. Cory in 1896. He first called it *Felis concolor floridana*. But since that scientific name was already taken by the region's bobcat subspecies, the name was later changed to *Felis concolor coryi,* in honor of Charles Cory.

▶ Cougar Subspecies

There are twelve known subspecies of cougar in South America and fifteen in North America, of which the Florida panther is just one. All cougar subspecies can interbreed but normally do not because they are isolated from each other by distance, mountain ranges, or bodies of water. As a result, each subspecies has developed its own subtly different physical characteristics over time. Each American cougar subspecies differs from the others in size, shades of skin color, and details of skull and dental structure. Most people untrained in biology would have trouble telling one sub-species from another. But it is important to conserve each subspecies, since each is unique to nature. Subspecies are protected under the Endangered Species Act of 1973.

▶ The Evolution of the Florida Panther

About 50 million years ago, a single evolutionary line of animals split in two and eventually evolved into today's cats and dogs. The first animals that we would likely recognize as cats are believed to have originated about 30 million years ago. These first small cats, known as *Dinictis,* evolved further, splitting into two branches, the huge saber-toothed Nimravids and the smaller, faster Felids.

▲ *One of the fifteen North American subspecies of cougars that is a close relative of the Florida panther.*

Smilodon were saber-toothed Nimravids with huge knifelike teeth 7 inches (18 centimeters) long, which they may have used to slit the throats of their prey. Saber-tooths inhabited North America until relatively recently. The saber-tooth branch of the cougar family went extinct at the end of the last ice age, about ten thousand years ago, and we know about these animals only through their fossils. Some of those have been found in Florida. Some scientists think that the last saber-tooths in North America may have been the victims of early human hunters who helped drive the animals extinct.

The Felid branch of the family, however, did not go extinct. In fact, the Felids have thrived and been very successful. Felid species are now wild on every continent except Australia and Antarctica. Between 10 million and 20 million years ago, the Felids also branched. The genus *Leo* developed into all of today's roaring cats, including lions, tigers, leopards, and jaguars. The other branch, known as the genus *Felis,* originally included all domestic house cats as well as smaller wildcats like the bobcat, lynx, and panther. In 1993, scientists reassigned the Florida panther to the genus *Puma.*

▶ The First Cougars

The first cougars appeared in North America about 2 million years ago. They have since

A North American cougar carries her kitten in the same way that a house cat carries her young—by the scruff of the neck.

developed into many regionalized subspecies. The fifteen North American subspecies of cougar were originally very successful in colonizing all kinds of habitat. That habitat ranged from the Appalachian Mountains in the east to the low deserts and high mountain ranges of the west as well as the hot, swampy, subtropical lowlands of Florida.

The arrival of European settlers brought hard times for cougars. Hunting by humans, loss of habitat due to development, mercury pollution, and other threats have devastated North America's cougar populations. Some, like the Eastern cougar in the United States, were thought to have gone completely extinct until recently. The highest populations of cougars today are in British Columbia, Canada, where roughly six thousand cougars live. In the United States, the highest concentration of cougars is in California. Three thousand to five thousand live there.[4] The Florida panther is the most endangered of the fifteen North American cougar subspecies.

▷ Historic Range of the Florida Panther

Before Europeans arrived in America, the Florida panther ranged throughout the southeast. It was found not just in Florida but also in Georgia, South Carolina, Tennessee, Mississippi, and Alabama and westward to Louisiana, Arkansas, and eastern Texas. At the western edge of its historic range, it likely

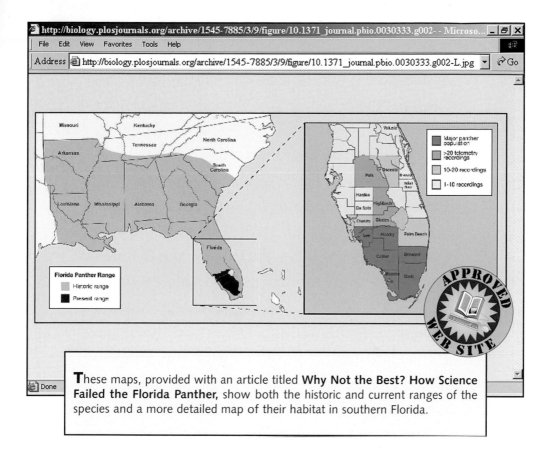

These maps, provided with an article titled **Why Not the Best? How Science Failed the Florida Panther,** show both the historic and current ranges of the species and a more detailed map of their habitat in southern Florida.

mixed with and mated with the Texas subspecies of cougar, *Puma concolor stanleyana.*

▶ Surviving in the Swamps: A Tale of Native People and a Native Animal

The Seminole Indians of Florida had great respect for the Florida panther, naming one of their clans for it, a clan from which their sacred healers usually came. The Seminole also believed the animal had great healing powers. Its tail and claws were thought to cure muscle disease while also increasing strength and endurance. Seminole children were warned to be silent in the evening so they would not scare off the panther's prey and give the village bad luck.[5]

Forced Into the Swamps

Spanish explorer Alvar Nuñez Cabeza de Vaca was the first European explorer after Columbus to see a Florida panther. He spotted it near the Everglades in 1513. But after him came European settlement and conflict that forced both the Seminole and the Florida panthers into the swamps of South Florida. The United States government waged three wars with the Seminole in the 1800s, and although the Seminole did not concede defeat, more than three thousand of them were forced to move to what was then Indian Territory, now Oklahoma. A few hundred Seminole, however, managed to escape capture by going to the remote swamps of southern Florida's Everglades where they could not be found. They are the ancestors of the Seminole and Miccosukee people who still live in Florida today.

Just as the drive for land in the southeastern United States affected a native people, it put tremendous pressure on the Florida panther, especially after 1850. The destruction of wilderness by human development left the panthers with few places to run. They vanished from one state after

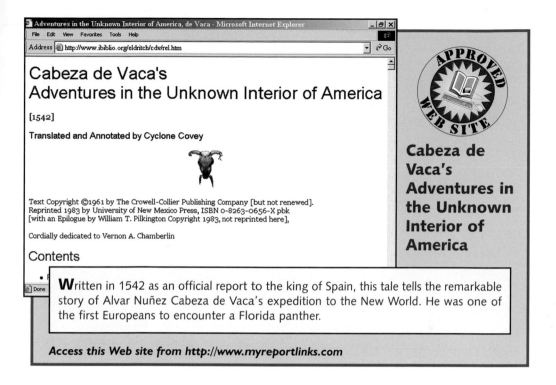

**Cabeza de Vaca's
Adventures in the Unknown Interior of America**

Adventures in the Unknown Interior of America, de Vaca - Microsoft Internet Explorer

File Edit View Favorites Tools Help

Address http://www.ibiblio.org/eldritch/cdv/rel.htm ⮕ Go

Cabeza de Vaca's
Adventures in the Unknown Interior of America

[1542]

Translated and Annotated by Cyclone Covey

Text Copyright ©1961 by The Crowell-Collier Publishing Company [but not renewed].
Reprinted 1983 by University of New Mexico Press, ISBN 0-8263-0656-X pbk
[with an Epilogue by William T. Pilkington Copyright 1983, not reprinted here],

Cordially dedicated to Vernon A. Chamberlin

Contents

Written in 1542 as an official report to the king of Spain, this tale tells the remarkable story of Alvar Nuñez Cabeza de Vaca's expedition to the New World. He was one of the first Europeans to encounter a Florida panther.

Access this Web site from http://www.myreportlinks.com

another, until the only place they could be found was Florida.

Over the years, the last Florida panthers were pushed farther and farther south on the Florida peninsula. The panther had pretty much disappeared from all of its northern range in Florida by the 1920s. The big cat continued to hold out in South Florida, which was then thought to be too swampy and mosquito-infested for people to settle.

Developers Discover Florida and Reduce the Panther's Historic Habitat

Early settlers first arrived in Florida after the Seminole Wars of the 1800s. Land developers and

The Big Cypress Preserve is one of the public lands in Florida where the Florida panther makes its home.

speculators then "discovered" southern Florida during the late 1800s, realizing that they could make fortunes in the Sunshine State. Ever since, the sale and development of Florida's lands have put the Florida panther on the road toward extinction. In the 1880s, oil tycoon Henry Morrison Flagler came to Florida and poured his fortune into developing the state's East Coast. He opened grand luxury hotels—some with more than one thousand rooms—from St. Augustine southward and eventually built a railroad through the Florida Keys all the way to the island of Key West.

More land developers came, converting vast areas of the South Florida wilderness into citrus groves, cattle farms, and housing developments.

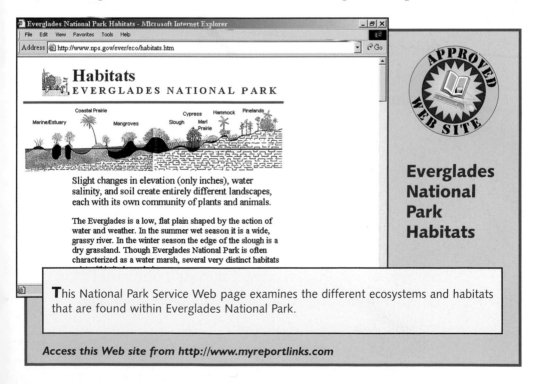

Everglades National Park Habitats

This National Park Service Web page examines the different ecosystems and habitats that are found within Everglades National Park.

Access this Web site from http://www.myreportlinks.com

All of this development put the Florida panther under greater pressure, and its numbers dwindled as it retreated into southwestern Florida. The founding of Everglades National Park in 1947 gave the Florida panther one refuge against approaching civilization. The Everglades' swamps, however, were not ideal for the big cats—panthers like drier high ground best as habitat. The construction of State Highway 84, now Interstate 75, known as Alligator Alley, which runs across the state and through the very heart of Florida panther country, caused more big problems for the big cats. The road not only opened the region to new development, but many Florida panthers were hit and killed by cars.

Shrinking Habitat

By the 1970s, the Florida panther's historic range had shrunk even more. It was pushed into the pinelands, hardwood hammocks, swamps, and grassy prairies at the southwestern tip of the state. Safety there was limited, however. These last panthers were within a half hour's drive of the bright lights, noise, and traffic of the huge city of Miami.

Today, the Florida panther has been cornered by human development. It occupies less than one percent of its original range, and its population is only between seventy and one hundred individuals, making it one of the most endangered animals in the world. Larry Richardson of the U.S. Fish and

Wildlife Service puts it bluntly when he says, "This animal is on a collision course with extinction."[6] Florida panthers remain critically endangered by human actions. So it is only through human intervention, with reintroduction, education, and outreach, that we can save them. Many naturalists and environmentalists are hopeful that the Florida panther can be saved—if enough people become committed to its rescue.

Home Range Today

An adult male Florida panther needs an immense home range—on average, 200 square miles (518 square kilometers) in the wettest parts of the Everglades. This range is larger than that required

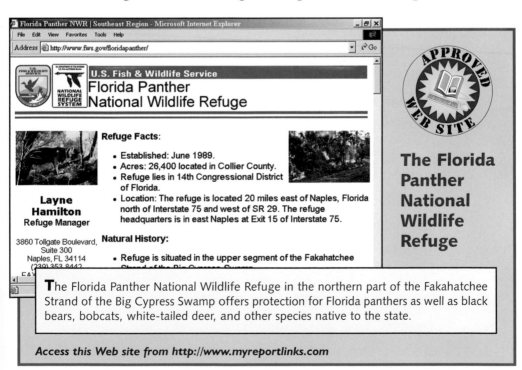

The Florida Panther National Wildlife Refuge in the northern part of the Fakahatchee Strand of the Big Cypress Swamp offers protection for Florida panthers as well as black bears, bobcats, white-tailed deer, and other species native to the state.

by any other North American cougar subspecies. In a study done on Texas cougars, they were found to need a significantly smaller range than the Florida panther. The need for such a large home range is linked directly to the poor quality of the South Florida panther habitat. Much of it is so swampy or has been so degraded by human development that adult panthers need to cover far more ground just to find enough food to eat.

The Florida panther today ranges over the 1,398,617 acres of Everglades National Park, the 729,000 acres of the Big Cypress National Preserve, and the 26,400 acres of the Florida Panther National Wildlife Refuge as well as in several Florida state preserves, including an important one along the Fakahatchee Strand. The big cat also roams over large stretches of private land that are covered in forests, ranches, or citrus groves.

The panther's range today includes a wide variety of natural habitats such as pinelands, hardwood hammocks, cypress swamps, freshwater marshes, mangrove swamps, and prairies. Unfortunately, much of the protected lands in South Florida are low wetlands. Few deer live in wetlands, and wild hogs are scarce in places like the Everglades.

How to Spot a Florida Panther

Though you are unlikely to ever come upon one in the wild, the Florida panther can be distinguished from other North and South American cougar subspecies by its tawny brown, relatively short fur—perhaps an adaptation brought about to deal with steamy temperatures in the southeastern United States.

Florida panthers are medium-sized cougars, smaller when compared to cougar subspecies in the American West. Male Florida panthers range from 99 to 154 pounds (45 to 70 kilograms), and females from 66 to 99 pounds (30 to 45 kilograms). However, many recently captured Florida panthers have been at the low end of these weight ranges, probably because of poor diet and other environmental pressures put upon them.

▶ Other Differences

At the shoulders, panthers can be between 24 to 28 inches (61 to 71 centimeters) tall, and they are typically 6 to 7 feet (1.8 to 2.2 meters) from the tip of the nose to the tip of the tail. The Florida panther's skull shape is one thing that makes it different from its western cousins. The Florida panther's skull is broad and flat compared to the skulls of other cougars. Also, its nasal bones have high arches. Like all cats, it has a short muzzle that allows its bite to be more powerful than that of a dog. The Florida panther has longer legs and smaller feet than western cougars. Florida panthers, like other cougars, have long, round tails.

Florida panthers can vary in color from pale brown or rusty-colored upperparts to dull white or buff-colored underparts. Their tail tip, ears, and nose are dark brown or black. When they are young, panther kittens have spots to camouflage them from other predators. The spots fade and disappear toward the end of their first year.

It was once believed that a crook, or right-angle bend, in the Florida panther's tail made

it different from other cougar subspecies. But scientists now know that the crook is a genetic defect caused by the inbreeding of the last few remaining panthers. It was also thought that the Florida panther could be distinguished from other cougar subspecies by distinctive white flecks around the head, neck, and shoulders. However, it is now known that these white flecks are caused by tick bites.

Even at seven feet in length, Florida panthers are smaller than the cougars found in western North America.

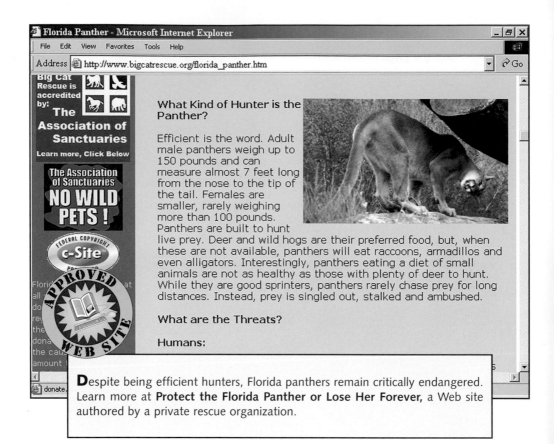

What Kind of Hunter is the Panther?

Efficient is the word. Adult male panthers weigh up to 150 pounds and can measure almost 7 feet long from the nose to the tip of the tail. Females are smaller, rarely weighing more than 100 pounds. Panthers are built to hunt live prey. Deer and wild hogs are their preferred food, but, when these are not available, panthers will eat raccoons, armadillos and even alligators. Interestingly, panthers eating a diet of small animals are not as healthy as those with plenty of deer to hunt. While they are good sprinters, panthers rarely chase prey for long distances. Instead, prey is singled out, stalked and ambushed.

What are the Threats?

Humans:

Despite being efficient hunters, Florida panthers remain critically endangered. Learn more at **Protect the Florida Panther or Lose Her Forever,** a Web site authored by a private rescue organization.

▶ A Fierce Predator

The Florida panther needs three key things to survive from one day to the next: plenty of space in which to hunt and breed, cover from which to stalk its prey and hide its kittens, and the prey itself—preferably big-game animals rather than small ones.

The Florida panther is a truly fierce predator. It is a carnivore, or meat-eater, and it kills almost all of its own food, though it sometimes eats carrion, or dead animals. While the panther historically ate white-tailed deer, it added wild hogs and armadillos to its diet when they were introduced to Florida's wild lands. Panthers also consider raccoons a choice food. Panthers will sometimes eat rabbits, rats, birds, and even an occasional alligator. One myth about the Florida panther is that it regularly kills cattle and other livestock. There are thousands of cattle in South Florida and only a few reported cases of panthers attacking them.

Panthers almost always hunt alone, though adult females may sometimes be joined in the hunt by their kittens. Florida panthers, like other cougars, rely on stealth and dense cover to sneak up on prey, which is why they hunt in the deep shadows of dusk and dawn.

Stalking Prey

You can learn a lot about how a Florida panther hunts by watching a domestic house cat as it stalks a toy mouse or ball of string. A Florida panther stalks its prey the same way. It creeps slowly forward on its belly until it is very close. Then it crouches and waits patiently, with its hind legs tucked underneath it, ready to spring. It keeps its eyes riveted on the prey, and when it judges the moment is right, rushes a short distance forward and pounces, drilling its front and back claws firmly into its prey. Florida panthers take white-tailed deer and wild hogs in much the

▲ *A Florida panther navigates the swamps of Everglades National Park.*

same way, by stalking them rather than trying to tire them out through a chase. When they are ready to pounce, Florida panthers can jump up to 14.7 feet (4.5 meters). With their front claws around the prey's neck and their back claws in its flank, panthers kill their prey with a fatal bite to the neck, cutting the spinal cord.

After the panther kills a larger animal such as a deer or wild hog, it drags the prey into the deep brush, where it eats the kill in private. What is not consumed right away, known as cache, is covered with leaves and twigs and saved for later. The panther will sometimes return for several days in a row to feed on the carcass. An adult Florida panther will eat 19.8 to 30.1 pounds (9 to 14 kilograms) of meat in one sitting.[7]

Asleep in the Shade

When it is not eating, the Florida panther does what most house cats do in the summer: It finds a cool, protected place to sleep. Panthers that are able to find large prey may dine just once a week and sleep for eighteen hours a day. Author Chris Bolgiano writes that while biologists are sweating and stomping through Florida's grueling 103°F (39.4°C) heat looking for signs of the Florida panther, the panther itself will likely be resting on a soft daybed, "hidden beneath head-high saw palmetto" at a much cooler temperature.[8]

Panther Reproduction and Life Span

Panthers are solitary animals. But that changes for a brief time when males and females come together to mate and produce offspring. The dense South Florida foliage and the elusiveness of the panther helped keep its mating habits secret

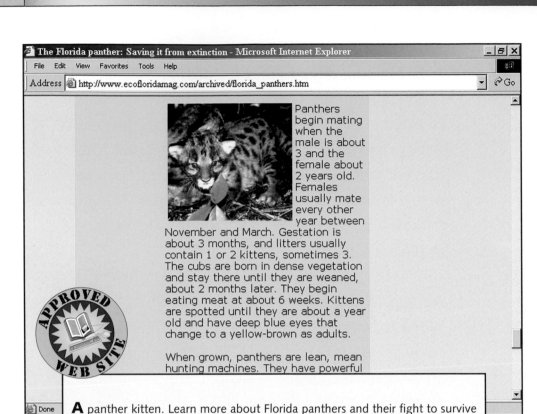

The Florida panther: Saving it from extinction - Microsoft Internet Explorer

File   Edit   View   Favorites   Tools   Help

Address http://www.ecofloridamag.com/archived/florida_panthers.htm

Panthers begin mating when the male is about 3 and the female about 2 years old. Females usually mate every other year between November and March. Gestation is about 3 months, and litters usually contain 1 or 2 kittens, sometimes 3. The cubs are born in dense vegetation and stay there until they are weaned, about 2 months later. They begin eating meat at about 6 weeks. Kittens are spotted until they are about a year old and have deep blue eyes that change to a yellow-brown as adults.

When grown, panthers are lean, mean hunting machines. They have powerful

A panther kitten. Learn more about Florida panthers and their fight to survive at **The Problem With Saving the Florida Panther: It's in Florida.**

EDITOR'S CHOICE

for many years. Scientists have slowly built up a picture of the big cats' reproductive practices.

Male Florida panthers mature sexually at about three years of age, and females mature when they are about one and a half to two and a half years old. When a female is ready to breed, she actively tries to attract a mate by caterwauling, a wild yowl that many people think resembles a human woman's cries. This yowl is what gives the panther its popular nickname *screamer.* At the Florida Panther Net Web site, you can even hear a female panther's yowl.[9] The female also can alter the scent of her urine, which signals a male that she is ready to mate.

The male and female stay together briefly at mating time, living and hunting with each other for about a week. During this time, the male panther will fight other males if they try to mate with the females in his range. Unlike some animals, panthers will have more than one mate in their lifetimes.

After mating, it takes about three months for a litter of one to four kittens to be born. While panthers can bear their young at any time of year, most do so in the spring when deer are bearing their

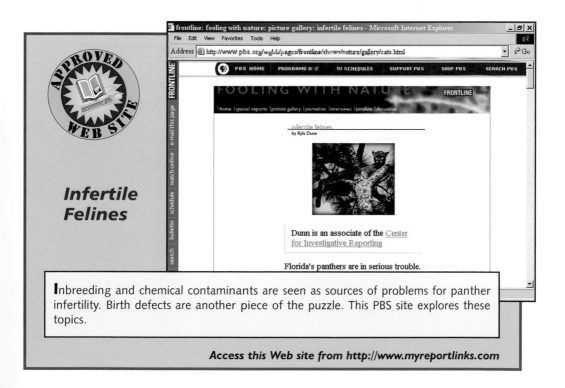

Infertile Felines

Inbreeding and chemical contaminants are seen as sources of problems for panther infertility. Birth defects are another piece of the puzzle. This PBS site explores these topics.

Access this Web site from http://www.myreportlinks.com

young. That is ideal for the female panther since she needs food for both herself and her kittens, and the defenseless fawns are easy to kill and provide a readily available food supply.

The male panthers play no part in the birth of the kittens. The female makes a secluded den in a palmetto thicket, settling in to have her kittens. The first couple of weeks after birth are a quiet time for the new mother and her young. She stays in the den much of the time, allowing the kittens to nurse. But the female must also leave the den to hunt for her own food, leaving the kittens vulnerable to other South Florida predators.

Kittens at Play

Watch domestic kittens at play, and you will get a good idea of how panther kittens act. They ambush, chase, and pounce on each other, playfully grabbing at each other's throats. While this behavior is fun to watch, it also trains the kittens to make their first kills. The mother takes the kittens with her to hunt when they are two months old. At first the kittens stay hidden nearby or watch. But by six months they have learned to mimic their mother and begin to become accomplished hunters.

The kittens leave their mother when they are one and a half to two years old, although why it happens at that age remains a mystery to

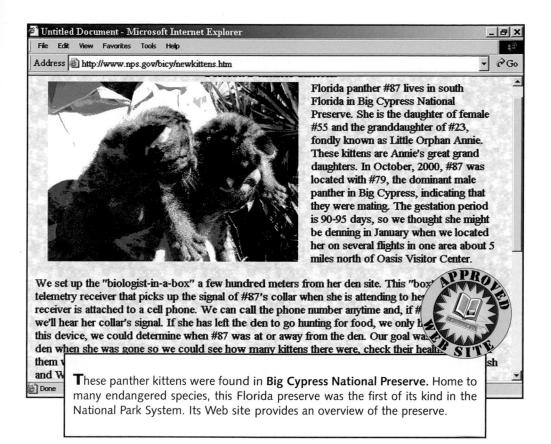

Florida panther #87 lives in south Florida in Big Cypress National Preserve. She is the daughter of female #55 and the granddaughter of #23, fondly known as Little Orphan Annie. These kittens are Annie's great grand daughters. In October, 2000, #87 was located with #79, the dominant male panther in Big Cypress, indicating that they were mating. The gestation period is 90-95 days, so we thought she might be denning in January when we located her on several flights in one area about 5 miles north of Oasis Visitor Center.

We set up the "biologist-in-a-box" a few hundred meters from her den site. This "box" telemetry receiver that picks up the signal of #87's collar when she is attending to her receiver is attached to a cell phone. We can call the phone number anytime and, if # we'll hear her collar's signal. If she has left the den to go hunting for food, we only h this device, we could determine when #87 was at or away from the den. Our goal wa den when she was gone so we could see how many kittens there were, check their heal them

and W

These panther kittens were found in **Big Cypress National Preserve.** Home to many endangered species, this Florida preserve was the first of its kind in the National Park System. Its Web site provides an overview of the preserve.

scientists. Mother and grown female offspring can live peaceably with overlapping ranges. But the juvenile males must fully separate from other male offspring, establishing their own ranges. The juvenile males are often forced out of their mother's range by larger, older, competing adult males.

▷ Life Span of a Florida Panther

Panthers in the wild live up to twelve years, although a panther was found in 1998 that was sixteen years old. Unfortunately, many panthers do not live to old age. The most common cause of early death is fighting between adult males and juvenile males. This might not be the case in a more natural environment. But the loss of panther habitat in Florida has resulted in male panthers being forced to crowd together into overlapping ranges. This overlap brings older and younger male panthers together more frequently than would happen under natural circumstances. The results are more battles to the death, with the males dominating a territory and its females. No one knows how long the life span of a Florida panther might be in the wild if there were fewer human-caused pressures.

THREATS TO SURVIVAL

Like so many animals and plants on the United States endangered species list, Florida panthers are not facing just one threat to their existence. They face many threats, most caused by humans. There are so few Florida panthers and the threats to their survival are so serious that even the failure to solve one major problem could doom the species.

▶ Habitat Loss

For more than two hundred years, the human population of the southeastern United States has climbed steadily, and with it, the population and range of the Florida panther has diminished. By early in the twentieth century, the panther was pushed back into its last safe haven in South Florida. But even there, what people called "progress" encroached on the big cats. Orange groves, cattle farms, cities, towns, suburban development, and new roads fragmented and degraded the panther's habitat. From the late 1930s to the late 1980s, a third of South Florida's

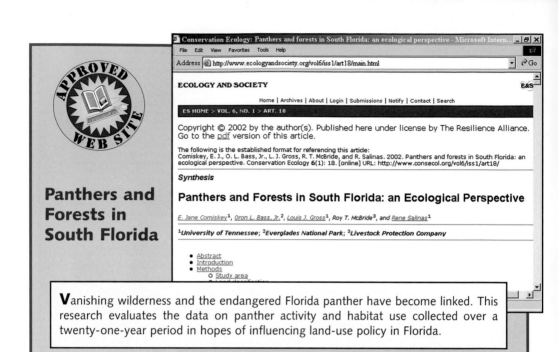

Panthers and Forests in South Florida

Vanishing wilderness and the endangered Florida panther have become linked. This research evaluates the data on panther activity and habitat use collected over a twenty-one-year period in hopes of influencing land-use policy in Florida.

Access this Web site from http://www.myreportlinks.com

forests were cleared for farming or for building homes. During roughly that same time period, South Florida's human population grew by nearly 5 million people, and the number of panthers continued to fall until only about thirty to fifty of them remained.[1]

The ongoing disappearance of prime Florida habitat means less of everything for the panthers: less cover in which to hide, less large prey to feed on, and less territory for adolescent panthers to claim for their own.

During the second half of the twentieth century, the panther did find some real safety in South Florida. Over that period, great gains were made in conserving public lands. The protection of the Everglades, Big Cypress National Preserve, and the Florida Panther National Wildlife Refuge offered hope to the remaining panthers. However, just because these lands were protected did not mean that they were not regularly invaded by humans. Florida panthers must share the Big Cypress National Preserve with hunters, trappers, and adventurers who travel on noisy and destructive off-road vehicles and on homemade swamp buggies, which environmental writer Chris Bolgiano describes as "a blend of tank and battleship—that smash through the thickest clumps of saw palmettos and slog through foot-deep swampy mires."[2] The panthers must also share the Big Cypress Swamp with natural gas drilling and mining operations. These intrusions can degrade habitat and put stress on the animals as they try to stay clear of human activities.

Reliance on Private Lands

Despite the large amount of public land in South Florida, the panther still relies on private lands for more than half its current range. Today, a good deal of these private lands are maintained as cattle ranches or for sustainable forest logging, low-impact uses that are mostly compatible with Florida panther habitat. Some of these landowners work with the government to try and maintain

http://edis.ifas.ufl.edu/EDISImagePage?imageID=307864986&dlNumber=UW202&tag=FIGURE 7&cred...

File   Edit   View   Favorites   Tools   Help

Address   http://edis.ifas.ufl.edu/EDISImagePage?imageID=307864986&dlNumber=UW202&tag=FIGURE%2078   Go

Done

Ranching brings hundreds of millions of dollars to Florida's economy. Many of the privately owned lands that support cattle, however, are also used by the Florida panther. At **The Ecology and Economics of Florida's Ranches** Web site, learn more about how good land stewardship can benefit both.

their lands as quality habitat so that Florida panthers will be able to continue to use them.

Unfortunately, the owners of these private properties are also under tremendous pressure to sell their lands to home developers. Five of the United States' fastest-growing cities—Fort Pierce and West Palm Beach on the east side of South Florida, and Naples, Fort Myers, and Punta Gorda on the west side—are sprawling toward the rural private lands where the panthers roam. A conversion of private lands from ranching and forestry to more intense uses such as vegetable farms and citrus groves is also taking away more panther territory. As a result, some key panther habitat disappears every day. If this steady loss of habitat continues, the last wild Florida panthers could go extinct within this century.

▶ Health Problems

The Florida panther is one of the most studied animals on earth. Its nearness to major cities and universities along with the concern by government and private conservation groups such as the Friends of the Florida Panther Refuge has meant a steady flow of research money to study the panther since the 1970s. Scientists now know that the panthers are susceptible to feline leukemia and other diseases as well as diseases caused by parasites. Panthers that are collared are vaccinated against these diseases and wormed as part of the management plan of the Florida Fish and Wildlife Conservation Commission.

The more that scientists learned about the animals, the more they saw how poor the panthers' health was. Loss of habitat results in the panthers sometimes not being able to find enough big game to eat. Even if they locate game, they can still become malnourished if they use more energy to find prey spread out over large areas than they get from the food they eat. This means that the

Biologists conduct a health exam on a Florida panther. The more that scientists can learn about the species, the better able they will be to help save it.

panthers that eat larger animals will generally be healthier than those who feed on smaller prey. To get the same nutrition that is in one deer, a panther would need to eat about ten raccoons. An adult panther needs to eat one hog or deer a week to stay healthy.

The panthers' constant need to search for scarce food while staying out of sight of humans also means that the animals are not able to live in their prime choice of habitat. Instead they must make do with whatever patch of wild land they can find. As biologist Dave Maehr notes, "The panther isn't truly a swamp animal. In fact, they disdain swamps as such. They stay out of them as much as they can."[3] Unfortunately, much of the remaining land available to the panthers is cypress swamp or other wetlands that offer meager food supplies.

Inbreeding and Dwindling Genetic Diversity

During the last half of the twentieth century, one of the biggest problems for the small number of remaining Florida panthers was inbreeding. When populations fall to very low levels, closely related individuals tend to mate with each other. When they do, their genetic diversity decreases with each new generation. A loss of genetic diversity means that each new generation of the animal loses some of its ability to adapt to its environment and is less healthy. Diminished genetic diversity for the Florida panther has led to lower reproductive rates, high death rates among kittens, and extreme vulnerability to diseases that a larger, more diverse population would probably have immunity to.

Until the mid-1990s, male adult Florida panthers had malformed sperm, which reduced the chances for fertilization of the female and increased the chances for birth defects. Heart defects never before seen in cougar populations killed panther adults and kittens.

▶ Extinction Vortex

Using statistics and computer models, scientists predicted in 1992 that without the introduction of genes from other cougar populations such as those in Texas or the western United States, the Florida panther's inbreeding would lead to the species' extinction within twenty-five to sixty-three years. Even a hundred total panthers, if completely isolated genetically, are not enough to assure long-term survival. This form of species decline brought on by inbreeding is called an extinction vortex. "Occasionally the jargon of science includes a term so elegantly succinct and expressive that no lay phrase can substitute," writes Chris Bolgiano in her book *Mountain Lion*. "Extinction vortex is one [such term], conveying an image of panthers

This tranquilized panther carried by a U.S. Fish and Wildlife Service employee has been banded so that its movements can be monitored.

sucked helplessly into a silent hurricane of genetic destruction."[4]

Fortunately, when biologists introduced eight female Texas panthers to South Florida in 1995, the animals mated with Florida panther males. Since then the number of birth defects and other genetic problems have declined, and the panthers' population increased from between 30 and 50 to between 70 and 100.

Mercury Contamination

Mercury is a toxic element contained in fossil-fuel emissions from power plants, incinerators, and the mining and metal refining industries. This mercury is released as fine particles and can travel long distances on the wind. Eventually, however, it settles to earth, polluting water and soil.

The danger of mercury poisoning to the Florida panther was discovered in 1989, when researchers studied a panther that had died mysteriously in Everglades National Park. The panther was found to have deadly levels of mercury in its liver.

The amount of mercury found in the air is not enough to kill Florida panthers. The mercury has to become concentrated as it moves up through the food chain for it to be deadly. Mercury emitted from factories and power plants is contained in rain that falls on wetlands and waterways. There it is absorbed by bacteria and algae that chemically

A great blue heron snatches a fish from the waters of the Everglades. The Everglades ecosystem is home to many species of plant and animal life, and all depend on each other for survival.

change the mercury, making it more toxic. The bacteria and algae are then eaten by zooplankton, small aquatic animals. The zooplankton are then eaten by fish and crawfish. Then the fish and crawfish are eaten by raccoons. Each move up the food chain further concentrates the mercury in the animal. Finally, the Florida panther eats the raccoon, getting a very high and deadly dose of mercury.

Mercury levels are lowest in Florida panthers that eat big prey such as wild hogs and deer that do not feed on fish. But the panthers that live in the poorer wetland habitats eat more small prey, especially raccoons that do feed on mercury-contaminated fish.

The only cure for this problem would be to reduce mercury emissions from factories, incinerators, and power plants. Unfortunately, the federal government, pressured by big business, has been pushing since 2000 to weaken mercury-emission regulations rather than strengthening them. Environmental groups are fighting the federal government in an attempt to make mercury pollution controls tougher.

Cars and Trucks

A major cause of death among Florida panthers has been collisions with cars and trucks. According to the Florida Fish and Wildlife

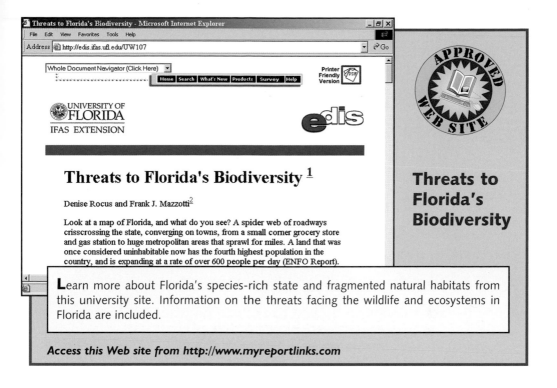

Access this Web site from http://www.myreportlinks.com

Conservation Commission, seventy-three panthers were killed on Florida's roads between 1972 and 2004, and the number of deaths per year has been increasing.[5] In the last few years, up to ten panthers a year have been killed in such collisions. The reason for this is that the panthers, because of their large home range, frequently need to cross South Florida's major roads in search of food, making them unintentional targets for fast-moving cars.

This problem is one that has not been fully solved, but it has been considerably eased by the construction of panther crossings, underpasses that allow the big cats to cross major highways safely and unseen. Protective measures have been taken along more than forty miles of highway that run through prime panther territory, including wildlife crossings and fencing. With these changes, the number of panthers killed by car collisions has been reduced to zero in these areas.[6] Unfortunately, the underpasses are very expensive to build, costing a minimum of $500,000 each.[7] Therefore, panthers must still take their risks crossing miles of busy highways. Lowered nighttime speed limits on some roads may have also helped to reduce panther fatalities, but those limits are not always obeyed. More government money is needed to build more panther crossings.

Hunting

During much of the past two centuries, the Florida panther was not seen as an animal worth saving but a pest that ate farmers' livestock. Scientists estimate that about thirteen hundred Florida panthers may have lived in the state before white settlers arrived. Many of those panthers were hunted and killed. Before Florida even became a state, its territorial government passed a law in 1832 that rewarded people for killing Florida panthers. In 1887, the state passed a law providing a five-dollar payment for panther scalps. Panther

▲ *People tour the Everglades on a jet boat. Tourism is a double-edged sword when it comes to wildlife: It brings needed revenue to places where endangered species like the Florida panther live, but it can also put animals at risk.*

hunting also became a popular sport among wealthy tourists from the Northeast.

The hunting of Florida panthers is now banned under the Endangered Species Act. That does not mean that they are completely safe, however. When an attempt was made recently to reintroduce panthers to north Florida, a few were shot by hunters.

The greatest danger that hunting poses to the Florida panther comes from habitat disturbance. Hunters who use off-road vehicles and swamp buggies to hunt white-tailed deer and wild hogs cause stress to the Florida panthers living in the area. Recent changes in off-road-vehicle rules and programs instituted on some federal and state public lands have somewhat lessened the danger to the panthers.

Bogged Down in Bureaucracy

The preservation and restoration of the Florida panther has been made more complicated by the number of overlapping state and federal agencies trying to save it. The Florida panther is protected by four government agencies: the United States Fish and Wildlife Service, the National Park Service, the Florida Fish and Wildlife Conservation Commission, and the Florida Department of Environmental Protection. These agencies try to coordinate their work through the Florida Panther Recovery Agency. Unfortunately, their well-intentioned efforts sometimes get tied up in red tape. Studies are commissioned, reports are written, and recommendations are made. But often it takes years for any of these recommendations to get funded and put to work in the field. Disagreements and competition between the agencies can make the process even more drawn out.

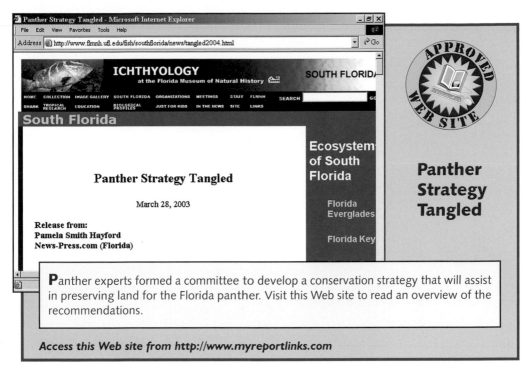

Panther Strategy Tangled

March 28, 2003

Release from:
Pamela Smith Hayford
News-Press.com (Florida)

Panther experts formed a committee to develop a conservation strategy that will assist in preserving land for the Florida panther. Visit this Web site to read an overview of the recommendations.

Access this Web site from http://www.myreportlinks.com

Ken Alvarez, a former government wildlife employee, is one of the strongest critics of the government bureaucracy's failure to protect the panther from the 1970s to the 1990s.

> [T]hose of us who have fed the hard years with cease-less labor at this herculean chore in Florida have seen our energies drained off in the sand. Every vibrant [Florida panther recovery] initiative is swallowed up by a leviathan of interlocked bureaucracies standing astride the path of change. Nothing can move if it is not in an officially sanctioned channel.[8]

▶ The Florida Panther Recovery Plan

Of course, many government officials argue that without the efforts of the federal and state governments, despite the bureaucracy, the Florida

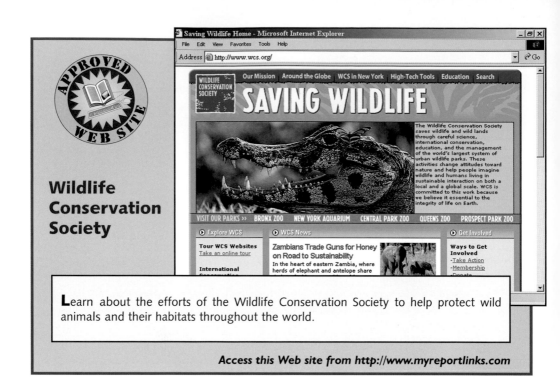

Wildlife Conservation Society

Learn about the efforts of the Wildlife Conservation Society to help protect wild animals and their habitats throughout the world.

Access this Web site from http://www.myreportlinks.com

panther would be extinct already. But often the efforts of those groups alone are not enough. Recently, more than thirty government agencies, private interests, and environmental groups came together to form the Florida Panther Recovery Team. In just six months, they drafted a new Florida Panther Recovery Plan with three main strategies to protect the animals and restore their population. First, they advised protecting the panthers and their habitat in South Florida and protecting and restoring travel corridors and habitat in central Florida. Second, they proposed establishing additional populations of panthers in the areas that were part of their historic range.

Third, they called for an education and outreach effort that will bring together the three groups involved to work cooperatively to save the big cats. The U.S. Fish and Wildlife Service is now reviewing the plan.[9]

Public Perception

No matter how successful a government endangered species recovery program may be, it depends on strong, active public support to keep it going. Many biologists are convinced that without constant public support, the Florida panther will disappear forever.

Such public support now seems to exist. Take, for example, a 1995 telephone survey in Florida. This survey found that 91 percent of the people polled would support any effort made to preserve the Florida panther. Among these efforts, 83 percent of those responding would support reintroduction of the panther into parts of its old range, such as northern Florida.

Unfortunately, it is easy to say yes to a phone survey. Things become more difficult and complicated when people are asked to act, to get involved, or to vote to increase their taxes to fund Florida panther protection.

Things also change when an endangered species program is seen to be affecting someone personally. Some people in North Florida, for

The reintroduction of Florida panthers in some of the areas of its historic range has met with opposition from people who fear the animal.

example, became opposed to the reintroduction of panthers in North Florida because of fears that the panthers might harm cattle, pets, or young children. Such opposition is known among environmentalists as NIMBYism, or "*not in my backyard.*"

Threats to the Endangered Species Act

The key to the protection of endangered species is the Endangered Species Act of 1973. Recently, however, some real-estate developers and large corporations have been pressing Congress to weaken the act or revoke it. The loss of the critical-habitat portion of the act could especially harm Florida panthers. Just as people cannot live without a home to shelter them or without grocery stores to feed them, endangered species need their habitats to survive. Quality habitat is the foundation on which endangered species like the Florida panther must build their recoveries. If the critical habitat section of the Endangered Species Act is abolished, many endangered animals could be put in greater danger of extinction in the wild.

Too Many Threats

The difficulty for the Florida panther is similar to the difficulty facing many other endangered species. The panther is not endangered by a single threat but by many different stresses brought on by the encroachment of human civilization on its habitat. Any one of the many threats facing the panther, ranging from loss of habitat to mercury poisoning, could lead to extinction.

To save the Florida panther and other endangered species we must look at environmental problems holistically. That means we need to look not at just one problem but at all the problems at once to see how they interact with each other.

Solutions must also be looked at holistically. If endangered animals are to be saved, we need to look closely at ourselves: at the houses we build, the cars we drive, the food we eat, and how much we consume and how much we pollute. The only way that panthers and humans can live together in the long run is for people to find an environmentally sensitive way of living that allows them to be comfortable but does not destroy nature in the process.

PROTECTING THE PANTHER

The Florida panther was first protected under Florida state law in 1958, the first such law to protect a subspecies of cougar in the United States. The U.S. Fish and Wildlife Service first listed the Florida panther as endangered on March 11, 1967, as part of the Endangered Species Preservation Act of 1966. When the Endangered Species Act of 1973 was passed by Congress and signed into law by President Richard Nixon, the Florida panther was added to the new and stronger law's list of endangered animals.

The Florida panther is also listed under Appendix 1 of the Convention on International Trade in Endangered Species of Wild Flora and Fauna (CITES). This global agreement protects an animal from international trade if that trade does harm to the species.

Unfortunately, adding a plant or animal to an endangered species list is much easier than actually saving the plant or animal. To do that, scientists must first gain a thorough understanding

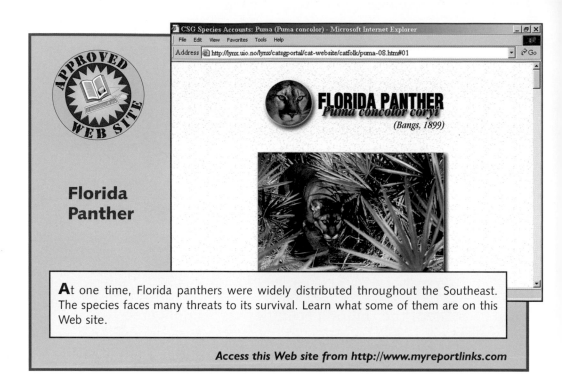

Florida Panther

CSG Species Accounts: Puma (Puma concolor) - Microsoft Internet Explorer

File   Edit   View   Favorites   Tools   Help

Address   http://lynx.uio.no/lynx/catsgportal/cat-website/catfolk/puma-08.htm#01   Go

FLORIDA PANTHER
Puma concolor coryi
(Bangs, 1899)

At one time, Florida panthers were widely distributed throughout the Southeast. The species faces many threats to its survival. Learn what some of them are on this Web site.

Access this Web site from http://www.myreportlinks.com

of the life cycle of the species and the factors that could be threatening it. Then they must work with government agencies to decide how best to save the species. This recovery strategy must then be acted on. Recovery can only happen if state and federal governments provide enough money to do the job right. Saving endangered species can be very expensive, and some people argue that there are other more important things we should be spending our tax dollars on.

The protection of an endangered species can fail at any of these steps in the process: Research may not be completed before a species goes extinct, or the researchers may not be able to determine exactly what is causing a species to decline. Even when this is known, many years can pass as scientists, environmental and wildlife agencies, and elected officials debate the merits of a recovery plan. The key to a successful recovery plan is public support. If people do not care enough about an endangered plant or animal to pay for the program needed to save it, then no recovery plan, no matter how good it might be, is likely to succeed.

The First Florida Panther Recovery Plan

In March 1976, a meeting at the First Unitarian Church in Orlando, Florida, led to the founding of the Florida Panther Recovery Team. This team was originally composed of biologists and other scientists from the National Park Service, U.S. Fish and Wildlife Service, Florida Park Service, and Florida Game Commission. Chris Belden of the Florida Game Commission was the first official to head up the recovery team. He was also the same scientist who fell out of a tree in 1981 while trying to protect a Florida panther from injury during its capture and radio collaring. Belden proved to be a good organizer and leader and a man totally committed to saving the panther. (In 2005, he joined the USFWS as a team leader with the Florida Panther Recovery Team in drafting its revised recovery plan.)

▲ *The Florida Panther Recovery Team has come a long way since the first panther was tracked, treed, and then captured so its health could be assessed. But there is still a long way to go in helping the big cats survive.*

The scientists knew that creating and carrying out a recovery plan for the species would be difficult. Ken Alvarez, a Florida state biologist, recalls: "We faced our job with some among us [still] unsure if there were panthers in Florida. If they could be found, the next question would be whether they were a remnant of the original wild stock, or captive pumas that had been released [by pet owners], or perhaps a mixture."[1]

For the Florida panther to be saved, biologists like Belden and Alvarez had to know how many of the big cats were left, whether they were able to mate successfully, and if those reproducing animals were descended genetically from the original Florida panthers. They had to learn what the greatest hazards were to the animals, develop a plan to reduce those hazards, and then somehow coax the species away from the brink of extinction. They also had to convince government officials and regular citizens to fully fund their effort.

By 1981, the recovery team had written and gotten federal approval for the first Florida Panther Recovery Plan. The plan included four major steps to save the panther. It called for providing and conserving the animal's South Florida habitat, the monitoring of the remaining panthers by radio tracking, the reestablishment of historic populations in places like northern Florida and Arkansas, and a Florida panther public-education program.

Controversy Over the Plan

Trackers including Roy McBride and his hunting dogs immediately went to work finding more panthers. They found adult males, females, and juveniles, which meant that a breeding population still existed, much to the scientists' joy. They radio-collared and then tracked every move of each newly discovered panther. Soon the scientists knew that there were only between thirty and fifty panthers still alive in the wild.

A Florida panther in the national wildlife refuge that bears its name. The animals use public and private lands equally, meaning that habitat loss and degradation is a constant problem for the species.

The scientists knew that, left on their own, these few remaining panthers would probably be the last. Only action by humans could save them. Unfortunately, when one tranquilized Florida panther suddenly died accidentally in January 1983, some Florida newspapers began to accuse the scientists of making a big mistake. The papers said that the researchers should not interfere with the wild panthers but leave them alone. The *Fort Myers News-Press* made this point:

> How can it help the few panthers remaining in the Everglades to be constantly tracked and trailed— on the ground and from the air—by wildlife officers trying to spot them, catch them and tag them with radio-signalling collars so they can be spied on the rest of their lives. . . . What the panthers need most is [to] be left alone.[2]

Successes and Failures

Despite such editorials, public support for what the scientists were doing grew, and their effort to protect the animals was never stopped. Between the 1980s and today, the recovery plan has met with real success. At the same time, some portions of the recovery plan have failed. Attempts to establish new populations of Florida panthers in North Florida and Arkansas failed to get public support and never happened.

The scientists had reasoned that if the Florida panther lived in at least three separate areas of its original historic range, the subspecies would be

The 2004 IUCN Red List of Threatened Species - Microsoft Internet Explorer

File Edit View Favorites Tools Help

Address http://www.redlist.org/

Introduction
Partners & Credits
Red List Programme
Data Organization
Summary Statistics
Sources & Quality
Categories & Criteria
Authority Files
Photo Gallery
References
FAQs
Links

The IUCN Species Survival Commission

2004 IUCN Red List of
**Threatened
Species**™

**IUCN Red List
of Threatened
Species**

SEARCH

EXPERT
SEARCH

The IUCN-World Conservation Union Red List is a searchable database of the world's endangered animals and plants. A summary of each species includes information on habitats and major threats.

Access this Web site from http://www.myreportlinks.com

more likely to survive for the long term in at least one of those places. Unfortunately, the Arkansas Game and Fish Commission rejected the plan to put panthers in their state at the time. There is still hope among conservationists that Arkansas will reconsider. An experiment that placed a population of nineteen sterile Texas panthers in North Florida's Osceola National Forest in 1988 and 1993 to see how they would do also failed when a misinformed public panicked.

"A father held his daughter in front of TV cameras and gushed about how he hoped to preserve her from being eaten," wrote environmental writer Ted Williams. "Deer hunters ranted to an insatiable press, and one, who had drenched himself with doe scent, reported that a panther had looked at him hungrily."[3] Hysteria existed even though there were no reports in the twentieth century of a Florida panther attacking humans. Two of the North Florida panthers were killed by poachers while another died in a snare trap. The state evacuated the remaining panthers, though nine died while being moved to other preserves.

▷ A Captive-Breeding Plan Is Proposed

In 1990, the U.S. Fish and Wildlife Service proposed a captive-breeding plan for the Florida panther. The idea was to take some Florida panther kittens out of the wild and let them grow to adulthood in the safety of zoos. When grown, the zoo panthers were to be selectively mated with other panthers that were distant relatives to avoid genetic inbreeding problems. The offspring of the captive zoo cats were then to be placed in the wild. Captive-breeding programs had worked before to save other endangered species including the red wolf, peregrine falcon, and black-footed ferret.

Captive Breeding and Reintroduction

Access this Web site from http://www.myreportlinks.com

Part of a larger work on biodiversity and conservation, this chapter sheds light on the many challenges involved in trying to save endangered species.

Critics of the idea raised difficult questions. They worried that such a plan had never been tried before with cougars and, that if it failed, it would remove too many kittens from the wild for no worthwhile purpose. They also wondered about what would happen if captive breeding was a big success. Without increased habitat in South Florida or elsewhere, there would be no wild place in which the estimated one hundred thirty to five hundred captive-bred panthers could live.

Problems With the Plan

The plan also met with problems when it was discovered that the panthers in Big Cypress and the Everglades were genetically different from each other. The Everglades cats had some Central or South American genes. The question was then whether the Everglades panthers should be protected at all under the Endangered Species Act, since they were not pure-blooded Florida panthers. The U.S. Department of the Interior decided that the Everglades cats still qualified for protection.

The Fund for Animals, an animal-rights group, fearing that kittens removed from the wild and placed in zoos might be harmed, sued the government and delayed the start of the captive-breeding program. In the end, the plan was never put into action, since a better solution was found: out-breeding, or genetic restoration.

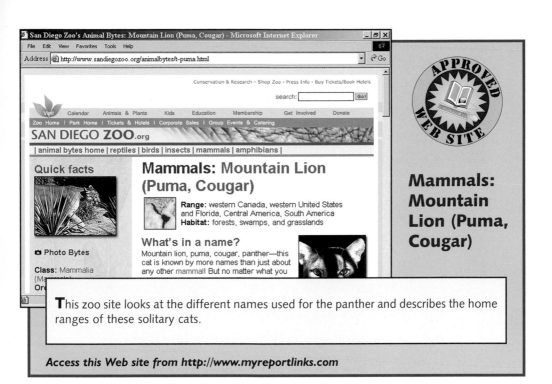

San Diego Zoo's Animal Bytes: Mountain Lion (Puma, Cougar) - Microsoft Internet Explorer

File Edit View Favorites Tools Help

Address http://www.sandiegozoo.org/animalbytes/t-puma.html Go

Conservation & Research · Shop Zoo · Press Info · Buy Tickets/Book Hotels

search: Go!

Visit   Calendar   Animals & Plants   Kids   Education   Membership   Get Involved   Donate

Zoo Home I Park Home I Tickets & Hotels I Corporate Sales I Group Events & Catering

SAN DIEGO ZOO.org

| animal bytes home | reptiles | birds | insects | mammals | amphibians |

Quick facts

Photo Bytes

Class: Mammalia
(Ma...)
Or...

Mammals: Mountain Lion (Puma, Cougar)

Range: western Canada, western United States
and Florida, Central America, South America
Habitat: forests, swamps, and grasslands

What's in a name?
Mountain lion, puma, cougar, panther—this
cat is known by more names than just about
any other mammal. But no matter what you

Mammals: Mountain Lion (Puma, Cougar)

This zoo site looks at the different names used for the panther and describes the home ranges of these solitary cats.

Access this Web site from http://www.myreportlinks.com

▶ Outbreeding Succeeds

One of the most important and successful steps taken so far to save the Florida panther began with a decision in 1994 to outbreed the big cats. A plan was launched that would bring female Texas panthers to South Florida to live and mate with male Florida panthers. The two are closely related subspecies.

In the spring of 1995, Roy McBride went to Texas and captured eight female Texas panthers. They were flown by jet to Florida and released into Florida's Fakahatchee Strand and Big Cypress Nature Preserve. The Texas females bred with male Florida panthers, and their kittens had enriched genetic diversity. As a result, many of the genetic problems that each new generation of Florida panthers had suffered, such as heart defects or difficulties in reproducing, began to disappear. Today's Florida panthers are the healthiest the subspecies has been since the recovery program began.

Some critics complained that mating Texas panthers with Florida panthers made the Florida panthers impure genetically. In other words, the resulting kittens were not true Florida panthers. But biologists argued otherwise. They said that before humans settled the Southeast, the Florida panther's historic range bordered the historic range of the Texas panther, so the two subspecies had once regularly outbred with each other. When one-hundred-year-old Florida panther pelts from museums were tested for genetics, they were found to have a percentage of Texas cougar genes.

▶ Wildlife Underpasses

Highways are a major killer of Florida panthers. The problem was especially serious along Interstate Highway 75, Alligator Alley, which crosses the state and cuts Florida panther habitat in half.

Starting in 1993, animal underpasses were constructed on Alligator Alley and then on Florida State Road 29, another location where panthers

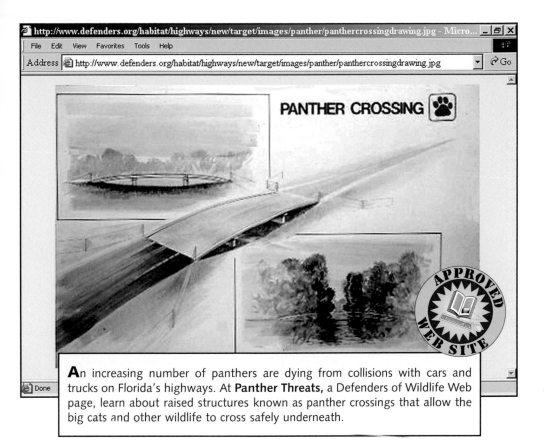

An increasing number of panthers are dying from collisions with cars and trucks on Florida's highways. At **Panther Threats,** a Defenders of Wildlife Web page, learn about raised structures known as panther crossings that allow the big cats and other wildlife to cross safely underneath.

had been killed. These panther crossings and tall fences along parts of the roads have significantly reduced panther deaths due to traffic in those locations. Reduced speed limits and "Panther Warning" signs for motorists have also helped cut collisions in panther country. These steps have not, however, eliminated the damage highways do. The volume of traffic and speed of vehicles on highways still limit panthers' movements and their ability to hunt or mate freely anywhere in their range.

▶ The Role of Preserves

Florida panthers require the largest range of any American cougar because the size and quality of their habitat has declined so drastically over the past hundred years. This decline forces the big cats to forage over increasingly larger areas to find enough food.

The federal government and state government have taken major steps to protect the panther's last refuges. On December 6, 1947, President Truman formally dedicated Everglades National Park, protecting "the spectacular plant and animal life that distinguishes this place from all others in our country."[4] The park, now nearly 1,400,000 acres, came just in time for the Florida panther, which had been driven into South Florida's swamplands. Had the Everglades been developed as citrus groves or cattle ranches, it is doubtful the panther would have survived.

Big Cypress National Preserve, adjoining the Everglades, was founded in 1974, the first preserve in the National Park System. Preserves differ from parks in how much of the land can be used for recreation. Today it consists of 729,000 acres of panther habitat including a mixture of pines, hardwoods, prairies, mangrove forests, and cypress swamps. While the preserve's habitat has been negatively affected by off-road vehicles and oil and gas drilling, the preserve might not even exist if it were not for the efforts of a small group of local citizens. They worked for years to stop it from becoming the largest airport in South Florida, proving that just a few people can make a difference when it comes to environmental action.

Other Refuges

By the 1980s, scientists realized that the swamp habitat of the Everglades was not ideal for

▲ *Big Cypress National Preserve exists thanks to a small group of concerned citizens who fought to keep an airport from being built there.*

panthers. The animals can find more game and hunt better in drier uplands than in wetlands. The scientists also understood that, even with all the added acreage of Big Cypress National Preserve, still more land was needed for the panther's range. In 1989, the Florida Panther National Wildlife Refuge was established. Today it includes 26,400 acres of prime panther habitat on the upper Fakahatchee Strand. "On a monthly time frame, 5–11 panthers use a portion of the refuge for hunting, traveling to other areas, loafing, or denning," reports the refuge's Web site.[5] The state of Florida has also protected significant panther habitat, including the 80,000-acre Fakahatchee Strand Preserve State Park and the 6,430-acre Collier-Seminole State Park.

▶ The Problems of Private Land

Despite all of the protected land in South Florida, the panther is not likely to survive without the conservation of the vital habitat that it uses on private lands. "We've done maps that show that fifty-three percent of the range occupied by panthers in South Florida is private land," Dennis Jordan, a former Florida panther recovery project coordinator, told author Chris Bolgiano.[6]

The panther's need for habitat on private lands is a big problem. Neither the federal and state governments nor conservation groups such as the Nature Conservancy can afford to buy all the private lands needed to protect the panthers. Many private-property owners do not want the government to interfere in the development of their lands, whether for housing developments, condominiums, vacation homes, citrus groves, resorts, ranches, or even airports. So far, local land-use plans and community zoning ordinances to regulate how people develop their properties have been ineffective in protecting sufficient private lands for the panther. If large-scale development on private lands is not controlled, the Florida panther could go extinct in this century.

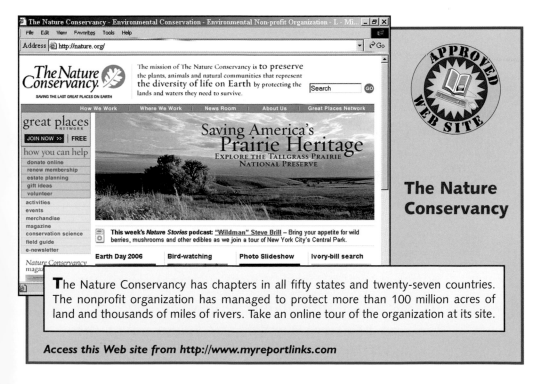

The Nature Conservancy

The Nature Conservancy has chapters in all fifty states and twenty-seven countries. The nonprofit organization has managed to protect more than 100 million acres of land and thousands of miles of rivers. Take an online tour of the organization at its site.

Access this Web site from http://www.myreportlinks.com

▶ A Plan Meets With Opposition

In 1993, a proposed federal and state Florida panther habitat preservation plan to conserve nearly a million acres of land, much of it now privately owned, met with strong opposition. Those most opposed were landowners, especially owners of agribusinesses—large-scale farming corporations. The plan proposed several ways to protect land, including purchase by the government, regulation of land use to prevent development, and conservation easements in which property owners voluntarily agree not to develop their lands in return for reduced property taxes.

David Land of Collier Enterprises, a large agribusiness company, complained to *Mountain Lion* author Bolgiano about the plan. "The [habitat preservation] plan even covers land where panthers have never been radio-tracked but where they could be reintroduced," Land said. "It's one thing when an eagle lands in one of your trees and builds a nest. But it's another thing when an endangered species is put on private lands and then use of those lands is restricted."[7] The plan was never put into place, and although it was replaced by another strategy, that plan was not adopted by the U.S. Fish and Wildlife Service. Until the thorny issues surrounding private-property land use and habitat are resolved, the future of the Florida panther will remain uncertain.

Public Education

Many researchers say that the key to saving the Florida panther is not more research but increased public awareness, interest, and action. As a result, the federal government and Florida state government, along with the Florida Panther Society and other nonprofit groups, are teaming up to educate people about the panther. Their goal is to teach everyone why the panther is important to Florida.

The Panther Posse

One of the most successful educational programs so far is the Florida Panther Posse. Forty Southwest Florida schools participate in this unique and exciting program run by Florida Gulf University's

▲ Florida's citrus growers bring billions of dollars into the state. Florida's agricultural needs must be balanced against the need for preserving habitat for the state's native animals.

Wings of Hope program and the Friends of the Florida Panther Refuge. Students who are part of the Florida Panther Posse help monitor radio-collared Florida panthers. A bulletin board at each school educates everyone about the panthers. Students also take the "Florida Panther Posse Challenge," which helps enhance their reading, science, geography, map, research, and ecology skills so that they can gain a better understanding of the challenges facing the Florida panther—and educate others. If the government and nonprofit groups gain enough strong public support for saving the Florida panthers, more money and energy will be put into saving the big cats. If enough people take an active role in protecting the Florida panther, its chances for survival will improve.

THE FLORIDA PANTHER TODAY

Even though the first Florida Panther Recovery Plan was launched more than twenty years ago, the Florida panther remains seriously endangered throughout its range. Despite successes with out-breeding, which resolved the panthers' genetic difficulties for the time being, problems continue to mount for these animals, whose habitat continues to shrink by 10 percent each year.

▶ Is Government Doing a Good Job?

Not everyone thinks that the government is doing a good job in its effort to protect the Florida panther. In 2000, major environmental groups including the Sierra Club, Audubon Society, National Wildlife Federation, and Defenders of Wildlife filed a lawsuit against the federal government for not taking adequate measures to protect the Florida panther. This lawsuit accused the government of allowing twenty-six real-estate development projects to proceed that would further shrink the big cats' habitat, in violation of the Endangered Species Act.

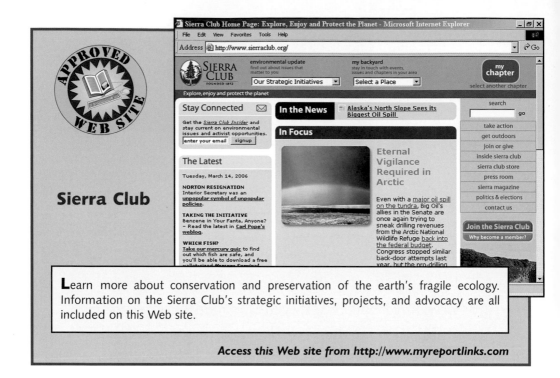

Learn more about conservation and preservation of the earth's fragile ecology. Information on the Sierra Club's strategic initiatives, projects, and advocacy are all included on this Web site.

Access this Web site from http://www.myreportlinks.com

Sadly, many of these new developments are named for the panther habitat they destroy. Take for example, the 584-acre Wildcat Ranch, the 196-acre Southern Marsh development, the 1,928-acre Winding Cypress development, and maybe the most ironic of all, a 1,000-acre development called the Habitat.[1] Some environmentalists have jokingly suggested that developers should be forced to name their housing subdivisions not for what they destroy, but for the harm they do to nature. These environmentalists think that if people really understood the damage that a particular developer had done to panther habitat, then people might not want to buy and live in the new houses.

During the administrations of George W. Bush, more than one hundred federal wildlife officials have expressed concerns that they could be fired from their jobs for trying to stop illegal or improperly permitted real-estate developments. They say that the administration is siding with the developers rather than trying to save endangered and threatened species, in clear violation of the Endangered Species Act.

▶ Speaking Out for the Panthers— And Losing a Job

In 2004, U.S. Fish and Wildlife Service biologist Andy Eller, who was with the Florida Panther Recovery Program, spoke out about the Fish and

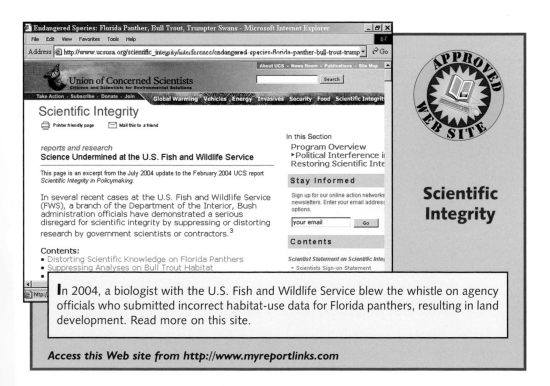

In 2004, a biologist with the U.S. Fish and Wildlife Service blew the whistle on agency officials who submitted incorrect habitat-use data for Florida panthers, resulting in land development. Read more on this site.

Access this Web site from http://www.myreportlinks.com

Wildlife Service's use of "flawed data" to measure the panther's habitat use and population. Eller reported that Fish and Wildlife had calculated the Florida panthers' use of habitat during the day, when the animal is usually only active at night; had supplied incomplete information that suggested the panthers used only upland habitat, when in fact they live in a wide variety of habitats; and had underestimated the number of surviving panther kittens. He himself included incorrect information in his reports when ordered to do so by his bosses. The miscalculations allowed a major development to go forward.

When Eller tried to correct the problem, he said, "I was ordered [by my superiors] to back off under threat of insubordination."[2] In November 2004, when Eller failed to back down, he was fired from his job with the federal agency.

▶ A Small Victory

In March 2005, the U.S. Fish and Wildlife Service conceded that it had used "flawed science" in assessing the panthers' habitat and population. In June, after a lawsuit, Andy Eller was reinstated by the agency, although he now works in Kentucky. Other legal victories in recent years by environmental groups in Florida have helped save land, but the battle continues.

▶ Do People Really Care About the Florida Panther?

Larry Richardson of the U.S. Fish and Wildlife Service defines the single most important problem preventing panther restoration today: "We know how to save panthers," Richardson says. "The problem is convincing the public we need to. This cat has to have habitat. If it doesn't, we're going to keep spending millions on a remnant population. And for what? To look at them in a zoo?"[3]

In the past nine years, the population of Florida panthers has doubled. But the animals have nearly run out of possibilities for expanding their territory. In fact, as their numbers rise, their habitat

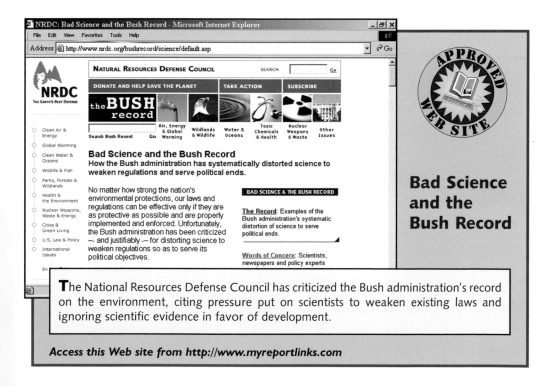

The National Resources Defense Council has criticized the Bush administration's record on the environment, citing pressure put on scientists to weaken existing laws and ignoring scientific evidence in favor of development.

Access this Web site from http://www.myreportlinks.com

continues to shrink. Unless Floridians become determined to find a way to protect more public land or habitat on private property, the Florida panthers' chance of long-term survival is not good.

"Floridians have come far since 1885, when they authorized a $5 bounty for each panther scalp," says environmental writer Ted Williams. "Now they support protection by purchasing Florida panther license plates. A professional hockey team has [even] taken the name of this erstwhile varmint."[4] In a recent survey, 91 percent of Floridians said they want to save Florida panthers from extinction. But wanting to do something is not enough. If people really want the panthers to be saved, they need to speak out loudly to state and federal officials who continue to support development over panther protection. "Just about everyone inside and outside the state loves Florida panthers. Until, of course, they interfere with business; then they're suddenly friendless," concludes Williams.[5] The public needs to decide finally whether protecting Florida panther habitat is equally important to building more malls, golf courses, housing developments, and highways.

▶ What You Can Do

There is much that you can personally do to help save the Florida panther. Most important, you can educate others about the threat to this big cat and encourage them to join you in saving this rare animal.

There are several nonprofit groups working to protect the Florida panther and educating others about its plight. By joining these groups, you too can lend your support to protecting panthers.

▶ Support a Panther Advocacy Group

The Florida Panther Society was founded in 1994. The group strives to protect panther habitat, reduce panther deaths on roads, and raise awareness of panther recovery needs including reintroduction

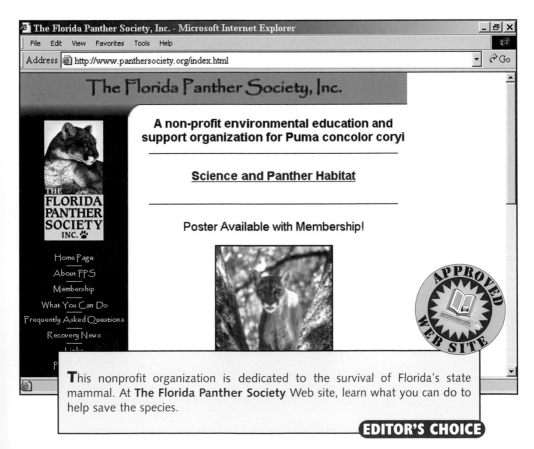

through public education and outreach programs. Their Web site suggests ways you can get involved, including writing letters to the wildlife officials who are supposed to be protecting the panthers, doing a school project on endangered species, and speaking out about what you have learned to educate others.[6]

Another group, the Friends of the Florida Panther Refuge, is an advocate for the Florida Panther National Wildlife Refuge. This organization tries to promote a better understanding and appreciation of the Florida panther, helping people learn how its existence enriches everyone's lives. The Friends of the Florida Panther Refuge have joined with the Florida Panther Society in its "Panthers and Pavement Program."[7] This campaign alerts the public and political leaders about the number of panthers that die on roadways. The group also promotes solutions to this problem.

Other Conservation Groups

Defenders of Wildlife is a national organization committed to saving endangered species. This group is working through its Habitat and Highways campaign to press for more panther crossings on major roads in South Florida. It also has an adopt-a-panther program that allows individuals or families to make a donation and receive a panther toy. The donation goes to help endangered panthers.[8]

Audubon of Florida

The Audubon Society, one of the largest and most important environmental organizations in the world, has state chapters. At the Audubon of Florida site, learn about local conservation campaigns to save Florida's wildlife.

Access this Web site from http://www.myreportlinks.com

Audubon of Florida has worked to get laws passed to protect the habitat of the state's endangered species including the Florida panther. It has also played a leading role in habitat restoration in the Everglades.[9] Habitat restoration is important even when land is owned by the government, because that ownership does not guarantee that the land is usable by animals for hunting or breeding. For example, degraded habitat that has been taken over by invasive species such as the melaleuca tree from Australia, provide little or no food for native bird and animal species such as white-tailed deer. Without white-tailed deer, Florida panther numbers drop. Restoration is an attempt to redesign the land, putting it back into its natural condition. Replacing invasive species with native species is a big part of restoration work.

Learn All You Can

The key to saving any endangered species is learning as much as you can about it and letting others know what you have learned. Perhaps you could combine learning with a vacation. A trip to the Florida Everglades or the Florida Panther National Wildlife Refuge would be fun and educational for your whole family, giving you a firsthand look at the wild lands in which the panther makes its home—if not the elusive animal itself.

If you are really interested in saving endangered species, you may want to begin thinking about a career in wildlife biology. Wildlife biologists such as Chris Belden and Roy McBride have been instrumental in the fight to save Florida panthers. They track the animals using radio collars, do other research, and write reports that inform elected officials how best to protect the species.

Organize Your Own Florida Panther Preservation Campaign

You could also organize your own Florida panther education and advocacy campaign. There are many ways to go about it.

The Panther Project | NIE WORLD - Microsoft Internet Explorer

File   Edit   View   Favorites   Tools   Help

Address http://www.nieworld.com/special/panther/   Go

NIE World Home   Teachers   Students   Families   > Projects <   Email NIE

The Panther Project

recover, monitor, protect

The NIE Panther Project has been designed for middle school and higher.

Recommended Links:
» Florida Panther Project
» Florida Panther Net

Males are the loneliest numbers

Big cats said to roam Volusia, but sightings unconfirmed

Panther conservation research center of heated debate

Panthers on the Prowl

Big cat's biggest needs — land, money

The Panther Gallery

Panther Sightings Map

APPROVED WEB SITE

The Panther Project

One of the basic goals of the Panther Project is to keep track of where Florida panthers roam. Sightings are tracked on maps, which you can view on the group's site.

EDITOR'S CHOICE

Access this Web site from http://www.myreportlinks.com

Give a presentation at your school about the Florida panther and the threats to its survival. Even if you do not live in Florida, the environment in your own community is probably suffering from many of the same problems that affect panther country, including the struggle to control urban and suburban sprawl, the loss of vital wildlife habitat, mercury and other forms of toxic pollution, and animal collisions with cars and trucks. You may want to compare these problems in your own territory with the problems faced by the Florida panther in its territory.

One way to build interest at your school is to work with your teacher to help launch a Florida panther or endangered species art contest. You can use the Friends of the Florida Panther Refuge poster contest as an example. More than five thousand students in southwestern Florida took part in this contest in 2004. The winning posters went on display in locations all over South Florida and can be seen on the group's Web site.[10]

You could also organize a class letter-writing campaign, urging elected officials and government wildlife agencies to take decisive action to protect the panther. The actions you could write about might include controlling suburban sprawl in Southwest Florida, increasing funding for panther research and recovery, and cutting mercury emissions from power plants. The Florida Panther Society Web site lists current contact information for political figures and wildlife agency administrators you could write to.[11]

▶ Help Protect the Endangered Species Act

The Endangered Species Act has helped bring back the American eagle, the symbol of our nation. It has also helped animals such as the green sea turtle and grizzly bear survive. But in recent years, some large corporations and developers have launched a fierce campaign against the Endangered Species Act. Though they call their ideas the "wise use movement," their program is misnamed. It is not meant to enhance our wild natural resources but to exploit and destroy them.

In 2005, the U.S. House of Representatives passed the Threatened and Endangered Species Recovery Act. Contrary to its name, however, the bill would do away with the critical-habitat section of the law and weaken it in other ways, too. If this bill or one like it is passed by the Senate and approved by the president, environmentalists will find it very difficult to continue to protect endangered species such as the Florida panther. Write to the president and your senators and congressional representatives and let them know that you do not want to see the Endangered

On the World Wildlife Fund's **Pennies for the Planet: Florida** site, learn how pennies add up to saving the Florida panther.

Species Act weakened. You can find the addresses for the president of the United States and members of Congress at Congress.org.[12]

Get Involved!

The years ahead will be challenging ones for the Florida panther and for other endangered species on our planet. Biologist E. O. Wilson warns us about the hazards we will need to confront:

> Now, more than six billion people fill the world. . . . Half of the great tropical forests have been cleared. The last [wild] frontiers of the world are effectively gone. Species of plants and animals are disappearing a hundred or more times faster than before the coming of humanity, and as many as half may be gone by the end of this century. . . . The race is now on between the . . . forces that are destroying the living environment and those that can be harnessed to save it. . . . If the race is won [against overpopulation and wasteful resource consumption] we will enter the future . . . with most of the diversity of life still intact. The situation is desperate—but there are encouraging signs that the race can be won. . . . Surely the rest of life matters. Surely our stewardship [of the earth] is its only hope. We will be wise to listen carefully to the heart, then act with . . . all the tools we can gather and bring to bear.[13]

The future of the earth is in our hands. All of us, working together, can make our planet a better place to live—not only for people but also for endangered species like the Florida panther as well.

HOPE FOR THE FLORIDA PANTHER AND HUMANITY

The state of Florida has lost one third of its forests and two thirds of its wetlands in the last sixty years. Since the arrival of European settlers, eleven species native to Florida have vanished forever, including the Carolina parakeet, the passenger pigeon, and the dusky seaside sparrow, which lost its habitat to the Cape Canaveral Spaceport. Today, 117 of Florida's species are endangered or threatened with extinction.[1]

Unfortunately, the rate of human development in Florida is proceeding at an incredibly fast pace, and habitat and wildlife conservation efforts have been largely unable to stop it. The future of the Florida panther and all the other threatened and endangered species in the state hang in the balance.

Their survival depends on the will of the people of Florida and the rest of the United States. If people really want to save the Florida panther, they will need to begin by changing their attitudes about the environment. We will all need to learn how to live cooperatively with nature, rather than seeing

The fate of the Florida panther lies in our hands.

nature as something to be feared, conquered, used, and abused.

▶ Respecting Wildlife

American Indians referred to America's cougars with names that showed how much respect they had for the animal. On the other hand, European settlers often gave scornful names to the North American cougar. The contrast hints at a basic difference in how primitive people and modern people regard nature. Ancient people lived in close contact with nature and relied upon plants and animals for their survival. Today's modern city-dwellers and suburbanites often forget that they too have a vital connection to nature and also rely on the environment to survive. Ancient people often worked consciously to conserve natural resources, while modern people often unconsciously abuse or waste them. The dirtying of our air and water; the destruction of our forests, wetlands, and other wild places; and the overconsumption of our natural resources not only threaten animals like the Florida panther—they also put our own species at risk.

If we are to save the Florida panther and other endangered species for all time, we will need to revise our thinking about nature. If each of us can learn to build respect for the environment into everything we do, from the moment we get up in the morning until we go to sleep at night, we will be much more likely to be able to heal our planet. If we continue to think that we are superior to and independent of nature, we could lose what little chance we have left to save all of our planet's beautiful animals—and we might lose ourselves in the process.

John C. Sawhill, the former president of the Nature Conservancy, said it best: "In the end, our society will be defined not only by what we create, but by what we refuse to destroy."[2]

In 1973, Congress took the farsighted step of creating the Endangered Species Act, widely regarded as the world's strongest and most effective wildlife conservation law. It set an ambitious goal: to reverse the alarming trend of human-caused extinction that threatened the ecosystems we all share.

Each book in this series explores the life of an endangered animal. The books tell how and why the animals have become endangered and explain the efforts being made to restore their populations.

The United States Fish and Wildlife Service and the National Marine Fisheries Service share responsibility for administration of the Endangered Species Act. Over time, animals are added to, reclassified in, or removed from the federal list of Endangered and Threatened Wildlife and Plants. At the time of publication, all the animals in this series were listed as endangered species. The most up-to-date list can be found at **http://www.fws.gov/ endangered/wildlife.html.**

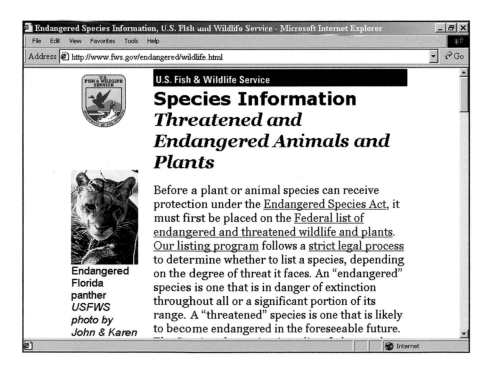

		STOP						
Back	Forward	Stop	Review	Home	Explore	Favorites	History

Report Links

The Internet sites described below can be accessed at
http://www.myreportlinks.com

▶**Florida Panther Net**
Editor's Choice The state of Florida offers this multi-resource Web site on the panther.

▶**The Florida Panther Society**
Editor's Choice This nonprofit group works to protect the Florida panther and its habitat.

▶**National Wildlife Federation: Florida Panther**
Editor's Choice The National Wildlife Federation offers an overview of the Florida panther.

▶**The Panther Project**
Editor's Choice The Panther Project works to inform young people about the animal and its plight.

▶**The Problem With Saving the Florida Panther: It's in Florida**
Editor's Choice *EcoFlorida* magazine explores the future of the Florida panther.

▶**Florida State Symbols: The State Animal**
Editor's Choice Learn more about Florida's state animal on this Web site.

▶**Audubon of Florida**
This site offers reports, photographs, and other resources on Florida's ecology.

▶**Bad Science and the Bush Record**
Learn about scientific integrity at the Web site of the National Resources Defense Council.

▶**Big Cypress National Preserve**
Visit the nation's first national preserve at its Web site.

▶**Cabeza de Vaca's Adventures in the Unknown Interior of America**
Read this full-text electronic version of a real-life Spanish tale of discovery.

▶**Captive Breeding and Reintroduction**
This University of California publication explores the problem of breeding wild animals.

▶**The Ecology and Economics of Florida's Ranches**
This University of Florida site examines the challenges of managing Florida's environment.

▶**Everglades National Park Habitats**
Learn about the variety of habitats that exist in the Everglades.

▶**Florida Panther**
The World Conservation Union discusses the fate of the Florida panther.

▶**The Florida Panther National Wildlife Refuge**
Learn more about a refuge for panthers and other wildlife in Florida.

Visit "My Toolkit" at www.myreportlinks.com for tips on using the Internet.

Report Links

The Internet sites described below can be accessed at http://www.myreportlinks.com

▶ **Infertile Felines**
This PBS article examines the problems that plague Florida's panther population.

▶ **IUCN Red List of Threatened Species**
This is a list of the world's threatened and endangered species.

▶ **Mammals: Mountain Lion (Puma, Cougar)**
The Zoological Society of San Diego presents information on mountain lions.

▶ **The Nature Conservancy**
This conservation organization works to preserve wildlife and conserve habitats.

▶ **Panthers and Forests in South Florida**
This University of Tennessee report on the Florida panther studies its habitat.

▶ **Panther Strategy Tangled**
Florida panthers and highways are not a good mix.

▶ **Panther Threats**
Defenders of Wildlife presents this Web site on panthers.

▶ **Pennies for the Planet: Florida**
This World Wildlife Fund campaign asks you to help wildlife around the world.

▶ **Protect the Florida Panther or Lose Her Forever**
Read about the fight to save Florida's state treasure, the panther.

▶ **Scientific Integrity**
The Union of Concerned Scientists reports how inaccurate science has undermined the panther.

▶ **Sierra Club**
This international group works to protect natural ecosystems around the world.

▶ **Threats to Florida's Biodiversity**
Saving the natural habitats of Florida is the focus of this article.

▶ **USFWS Endangered Species Program Kids Corner**
This USFWS Web page offers ways you can help save endangered species.

▶ **Why Not the Best? How Science Failed the Florida Panther**
Read how the peer-review process failed the Florida panther.

▶ **Wildlife Conservation Society**
This nonprofit fights to protect the wildlife and wild lands of the world.

captive breeding—Removing individual animals of an endangered species from the wild, breeding them in zoos, and returning their offspring to the wild.

carnivore—A meat-eating animal.

carrion—The flesh of dead animals eaten by carnivores or omnivores.

charismatic megafauna—Big animals that are few in number and on the brink of extinction that attract public sympathy, attention, and support for preservation.

critical habitat—Under the Endangered Species Act, the entire functioning ecosystem in which an endangered animal lives.

current range—The territory which a species or subspecies inhabits today.

diminished genetic diversity—The impoverishing of a species' (or subspecies') gene pool that results in the species losing its ability to adapt to its environment and stay healthy. Diminished genetic diversity is caused when a tiny remnant population of the species or subspecies inbreeds.

genetic restoration—This recovery strategy, also called outbreeding, mates an endangered animal subspecies with another subspecies in the wild to enrich its genetic diversity, preventing birth defects and other inbreeding problems. Florida panthers were successfully mated with Texas panthers.

gestation—The mother's carrying of her offspring, usually expressed in the time from conception to birth.

habitat—The area in which a species lives.

habitat generalist—An animal such as the Florida panther that can live in different habitats.

hardwood hammock—An upland "island" covered with trees and surrounded on all sides by wetlands.

historic range—The territory which a species or subspecies inhabited before modern humans arrived on the scene.

home range—The range of an individual animal.

NIMBYism—(abbreviation for "Not In My Back Yard") The opposition of a group to something being located close to it, such as people opposing a construction project or environmental program in their neighborhood.

sloughs—(pronounced *slews*) Winding streams and shallow pockets of water in swampy areas.

subspecies—A portion of a species that, due to its isolation, has evolved different physical characteristics from the rest of the species. Despite these physical differences, a subspecies can still interbreed successfully with other members of its species, but usually does not. Subspecies are protected under the Endangered Species Act.

tree (verb)—To drive toward or up a tree.

Chapter 1. The Race to Save the Florida Panther

1. Charles Fergus, *Swamp Screamer* (Gainesville: University Press of Florida, 1998), pp. 10–11.

2. Robert H. Busch, *The Cougar Almanac* (Guilford, Conn.: The Lyons Press, 2004), p. 110.

3. Ken Alvarez, *Twilight of the Panther* (Sarasota, Fla.: Myakka River Publishing, 1993), p. 69.

4. Fergus, p. 23.

5. State of Florida, Florida Panther Net, *Range of Cougar,* n.d., <http://www.panther.state.fl.us/handbook/natural/range cougar.html> (November 17, 2005).

6. Kirk Nielsen, "Slaughter Alley, Big Dead Cats in the Middle of the Road—Lots of Them," *Miami New Times,* June 14, 2001, <http://www.miaminewtimes.com/issues/2001-06-14/metro .html> (November 17, 2005).

7. Fergus, p. 197.

8. Ibid., p. 202.

9. Ibid., p. 208.

Chapter 2. All About Florida's Big Cat

1. Robert H. Busch, *The Cougar Almanac* (Guilford, Conn.: The Lyons Press, 2004), p. 16.

2. State of Florida, Florida Panther Net, *What's in a Name,* n.d., <http://www.panther.state.fl.us/handbook/natural/what name.html> (November 17, 2005).

3. Busch, p. 16.

4. Ibid., p. 25.

5. State of Florida, Florida Panther Net, *What's in a Name,* n.d., <http://www.panther.state.fl.us/handbook/natural/what name.html> (November 17, 2005).

6. Ted Williams, "Going Catatonic," *Audubon,* September– October 2004, p. 22.

7. State of Florida, Florida Panther Net, *Hunting Methods,* n.d., <http://www.panther.state.fl.us/handbook/natural/hunting .html> (November 17, 2005).

8. Chris Bolgiano, *Mountain Lion, An Unnatural History of Pumas and People* (Mechanicsburg, Pa.: Stackpole Books, 2001), p. 137.

9. State of Florida, Florida Panther Net, *Mating and Reproduction,* n.d., <http://www.panther.state.fl.us/handbook /natural/mating.html> (November 17, 2005).

Chapter 3. Threats to Survival

1. State of Florida, Florida Panther Net, *Habitat Loss,* n.d., <http://www.panther.state.fl.us/handbook/threats/loss.html> (November 17, 2005).

2. Chris Bolgiano, *Mountain Lion, An Unnatural History of Pumas and People* (Mechanicsburg, Pa.: Stackpole Books, 2001), p. 140.

3. Robert H. Busch, *The Cougar Almanac* (Guilford, Conn.: The Lyons Press, 2004), p. 109.

4. Bolgiano, p. 146.

5. Comments from Karen Hill, president, Florida Panther Society, Inc., January 22, 2006, in her capacity as advisor to this book.

6. Florida Fish and Wildlife Conservation Commission Bureau of Wildlife Diversity Conservation, *A Summary of Florida Panther Mortality Caused by Vehicular Collisions,* July 13, 2001, p. 1.

7. Ibid.

8. Ken Alvarez, *Twilight of the Panther* (Sarasota, Fla.: Myakka River Publishing, 1993), p. 447.

9. Comments from Karen Hill, president, Florida Panther Society, Inc., January 22, 2006, in her capacity as advisor to this book.

Chapter 4. Protecting the Panther

1. Ken Alvarez, *Twilight of the Panther* (Sarasota, Fla.: Myakka River Publishing, 1993), p. 63.

2. Ibid., p. 73.

3. Ted Williams, "Going Catatonic," *Audubon,* September–October 2004, p. 30.

4. National Park Service, Official Web site of Everglades National Park, *Park Establishment, Everglades National Park,* n.d., <http://www.nps.gov/ever/eco/nordeen.htm (November 19, 2005).

5. U.S. Fish and Wildlife Service, *Florida Panther National Wildlife Refuge,* n.d., <http://www.fws.gov/floridapanther/> (November 19, 2005).

6. Chris Bolgiano, *Mountain Lion, An Unnatural History of Pumas and People* (Mechanicsburg, Pa.: Stackpole Books, 2001), p. 150.

7. Ibid., p. 155.

Chapter 5. The Florida Panther Today

1. Ted Williams, "Going Catatonic," *Audubon,* September–October 2004, p. 24.

2. Ibid.

3. Ibid.

4. Ibid., p. 29.

5. Ibid.

6. The Florida Panther Society, Inc., *What You Can Do,* n.d., <http://www.panthersociety.org/what.html> (November 19, 2005).

7. Friends of the Florida Panther Refuge, *Panthers and Pavement,* n.d., <http://www.floridapanther.org/panthers-pave ment-march.htm> (November 19, 2005).

8. Defenders of Wildlife, *Wildlife Adoption Center,* n.d., <http://defenders.spacely.com/DirectedGiving/DirectedGiving .cfm?ID=113&c=5&orgid=hadopto> (November 19, 2005).

9. Audubon of Florida, *Everglades Restoration,* n.d., <http://www.audubonofflorida.org/science/everglades.htm> (November 19, 2005).

10. Friends of the Florida Panther Refuge, *Poster Contest,* n.d., <http://www.floridapanther.org/poster-awards.htm> (November 19, 2005).

11. The Florida Panther Society, Inc., *What You Can Do,* n.d., <http://www.panthersociety.org/what.html> (November 19, 2005).

12. Congress.org, n.d., <http://www.congress.org/ congressorg/home/> (March 6, 2006).

13. Edward O. Wilson, *The Future of Life* (New York: Alfred A. Knopf, 2002), p. xxii.

Chapter 6. Hope for the Florida Panther and Humanity

1. Charles Fergus, *Swamp Screamer* (Gainesville: University Press of Florida, 1998), p. 169.

2. Edward O. Wilson, *The Future of Life* (New York: Alfred A. Knopf, 2002), inscription.

Becker, John E. *The Florida Panther.* San Diego: KidHaven Press, 2003.

Busch, Robert H. *The Cougar Almanac: A Complete Natural History of the Mountain Lion.* New York: Lyons Press, 2004.

Butcher, Russell D. *America's National Wildlife Refuges.* Lanham, Md.: Roberts Rinehart Publishers, 2003.

Few, Roger. *Animal Watch.* New York: DK, 2001.

Gaughen, Shasta, ed. *Endangered Species.* San Diego: Greenhaven Press, 2006.

Grunwald, Michael. *The Swamp: The Everglades, Florida, and the Politics of Paradise.* New York: Simon and Schuster, 2006.

Hamilton, John. *Everglades National Park.* Edina, Minn.: ABDO Publishing Co., 2005.

Maehr, David S. *The Florida Panther: Life and Death of a Vanishing Carnivore.* Washington, D.C.: Island Press, 1997.

Pringle, Laurence. *The Environmental Movement: From Its Roots to the Challenges of a New Century.* New York: HarperCollins, 2000.

Silverstein, Alvin, Virginia Silverstein, and Laura Silverstein Nunn. *The Florida Panther.* Brookfield, Conn.: Millbrook Press, 1997.

Thomas, Peggy. *Big Cat Conservation.* Brookfield, Conn.: Twenty-First Century Books, 2000.

A

Alligator Alley, 42, 90
Alvarez, Ken, 13–14, 72, 82
Audubon of Florida, 107

B

Belden, Chris, 14, 81, 108
Big Cypress National Preserve, 40, 43, 44, 55, 59, 92–93
birth defects, 53, 64
Bolgiano, Chris, 59, 64
breeding habits, 51–54
bureaucracy as threat, 72–73, 99–101

C

Cabeza de Vaca, Alvar Nuñez, 38, 39
captive-breeding plan, 87–88
charismatic megafauna, 18–19
classification, taxonomic, 31–32
Collier-Seminole State Park, 94
Columbus, Christopher, 31
Convention on International Trade in Endangered Species of Wild Flora and Fauna (CITES), 79
Cory, Charles B., 31, 32
cougars, 29–32, 34–36

D

Defenders of Wildlife, 106
development, 38–43, 57–59, 95–96, 99–104
diet, 6, 7, 48–51, 63
Dinictis, 33
discovery of Florida panther
about, 31, 38
naming and, 31–32
and research, 13–15

E

education, 97–98, 104–105, 108
Eller, Andrew, 101–102
Endangered Species Act of 1973
Florida panther, inclusion of, 9, 79
habitat protection by, 22
passage of, 7
protection of, 26, 77, 110–112
subspecies under, 32
Endangered Species Preservation Act of 1966, 7, 79
Everglades National Park, 41, 42, 44, 59, 67, 92
evolution, 33–36
extinction vortex, 64, 66, 78, 113

F

facts about Florida panthers, 6–7
Fakahatchee Strand State Preserve
described, 11–13
as Florida panther refuge, 43, 44, 94
as human refuge, 26
Felids, 33, 34
feline leukemia, 61
Felis concolor, 31
Felis genus, 34
Fergus, Charles, 8, 26–28
Flagler, Henry Morrison, 41
Florida Audubon Society, 17
Florida Department of Environmental Protection, 72
Florida Department of Natural Resources, 17
Florida Fish and Wildlife Conservation Commission, 61, 68–69, 72
Florida Game Commission, 17
Florida panther
described, 6, 15, 29–30, 44–47
as endangered species, 18, 36, 99
as umbrella species, 19, 24
Florida Panther National Wildlife Refuge, 43, 44, 59, 94
Florida Panther Posse, 97–98
Florida Panther Recovery Agency, 72, 81
Florida Panther Recovery Plan, 73–75, 81–85
Florida Panther Society, 17, 26, 97, 105–106
food chains
as indicators of healthy ecosystems, 22–24
poisoning via, 66, 68
Friends of the Florida Panther Refuge, 26, 61, 98, 106
Fund for Animals, 88

G

genetic diversity, 63–64, 88, 90
gestation period, 7, 53

H

habitat
of Florida panther, 6, 38–39
protection of, 19–24, 74, 96, 103–105, 107
restoration of, 107–108

in species recovery, 77
swamps as, 21, 38–39, 42, 63,
92–94
habitat loss. *See also* development.
consequences of, 21, 23–24
and food supply, 61
government in, 99, 102
prevention of, 25–26
as threat, 23–24, 36, 38–43,
57–59, 84
healing powers, 37–38
health issues, 61–63, 90
heart defects, 64, 90
highways, 42, 90. *See also* vehicles.
how to help this species survive.
See also threats to survival.
citizen actions, 24–26, 43, 75, 77,
108–116
education, 97–98, 104–105,
108–110
habitat, protection of, 19–24, 74,
96, 103–105, 107
human activities, 57–59, 70–72, 113.
See also development.
hunting
of Florida panthers by humans,
70–72
habits of Florida panthers,
48–51, 54

I
inbreeding, 47, 53, 63–64, 87
Interstate 75, 42, 90
IUCN-World Conservation Union
Red List, 86

J
job loss, 101–102
Jordan, Dennis, 94

K
kittens
birth of, 53–54
in captive-breeding plans, 87–88
described, 46
in hunting, 49
maturation, age at, 7, 52
at play, 54–55

L
leisure habits, 51
Leo genus, 34
life span, 7, 55–56

Linnaeus, Carolus, 31–32
litter size, 7

M
Maehr, Dave, 63
malnutrition, 23–24, 61, 63
mating habits, 51–54.
See also gestation period.
maturity, time to, 7, 52
McBride, Roy, 9–11, 14, 15, 83, 89, 108
mercury poisoning, 24, 36, 66, 68
Miccosukee Indians, 38
Mountain Lion (Bolgiano), 64

N
National Park Service, 17, 72
nature, respect for, 115–116
Nature Conservancy, 95
NIMBYism, 77
Nimravids, 33, 34

O
off-road vehicles, 59, 72
Olson, Dennis, on healthy habitats, 22
outbreeding, 89–90

P
Panther Project, 109
parasites, 61
pollutants, 24, 36, 53, 66, 68, 115
population
counting, 15–16
establishment of, 74, 76
statistics, 7, 18, 36, 103
preservation. *See also* protection.
early efforts, 16–18
reasons for, 18–19, 22, 26–28
preserves, role of, 92–94
private lands as range, 59–61, 94–96
protection. *See also* Florida Panther
Recovery Plan; preservation.
about, 9–11, 79–81, 85–87
from collisions, 69–70
dates of, 7, 79
education and, 97–98
job loss and, 101–102
and public opinion, 103–104
public opinion and protection,
103–104
Puma concolor, 31, 34.
See also Florida panther.
Puma concolor stanleyana, 37, 43,
66, 89

R

radio tracers, 15, 65, 83, 85
ranching, 60
range
    current, 6, 22, 43–44
    historic, 36–37
    maps, 5, 37
    overlapping, 55, 56
    private lands as, 59–61, 94–96
recovery, 80–81. *See also* Florida
    Panther Recovery Plan.
reproduction, 51–54. *See also*
    gestation period.
research
    about, 11–13, 61
    Florida panther discovery, 13–15
respect for wildlife, 115–116
Richardson, Larry, 24, 42–43

S

saber-tooths, 34
Seminole Indians, 29, 37, 38
Smilodon, 34
Solitary Spirits (Olson), 22
State Highway 84, 42
subspecies of cougars, 32, 36
swamp buggies, 59, 72
swamps as habitat, 21, 38–39, 42,
    63, 92–94
Swamp Screamer (Fergus), 26

T

Texas cougars, 37, 43, 66, 89
The Twilight of the Panther (Alvarez),
    13–14
Threatened and Endangered Species
    Recovery Act, 111
threats to survival. *See also* how to
    help this species survive.
    bureaucracy, 72–73, 99–101
    development, 38–42, 57–59,
        95–96, 99–104
    habitat loss, 23–24, 36, 38–43,
        57–59, 84
    health issues, 61–63, 90
    highways, 42, 90
    human activities, 57–59, 70–72, 113
    hunting, 70–72
    list of, 7, 16, 36
    malnutrition, 23–24, 61, 63
    mercury poisoning, 24, 36, 66, 68
    pollutants, 24, 36, 53, 66, 68, 115

    quantity, 77–78
    vehicles, 68–70, 90–91
tourism, 71
tracking Florida panthers, 15, 65,
    83, 85

U

umbrella species, 19, 24
underpasses, 69, 70, 90–91
U.S. Fish and Wildlife Service
    captive-breeding plan, 87–88
    in Florida panther preservation,
        17, 25, 72, 79, 96
    and habitat loss, 102

V

vehicles, 68–70, 90–91

W

World Wildlife Fund, 9

Y

yowling, 52–53